THE TEENAGER AND THE LAW

THE TEENAGER AND THE LAW

By

ALBERT L. AYARS
and
JOHN M. RYAN

THE CHRISTOPHER PUBLISHING HOUSE
NORTH QUINCY, MASSACHUSETTS

PRINTED IN
THE UNITED STATES OF AMERICA

Dedicated to the Nation's youth
in whose hands resides the
fate of our future.

PREFACE

"Write a little book about the interests of youth and how they are related to the law." Externally, we nodded and smiled. Inwardly, we winced a bit at the publisher's terminology, "little book," considering how many local, state and federal laws there are and that there are nearly 30 million teenage youths running around. One seventh of the nation's total population is between the ages of 13 and 19. How many thousands of laws there are we can't say, but most of them apply in one way or another to those 30 million youths.

However, it is possible to cite classifications of law which have the most direct impact on people in the teen years and still keep the book small. So that's what we set out to do.

Laws, generally speaking, exist to help people in their relationships with each other, so they won't be deprived of safety, property, rights and opportunities. Laws are needed to enable young people, and everybody else, to get to where they want to go and do what they want to do—at home, in school, in later life—the whole thing—so long as they don't deny others similar privileges. Obviously, my co-author, John Ryan, a successful lawyer, is chiefly responsible for the legal interpretations included in the book. I thank him.

Albert L. Ayars

Writing a book for a particular age group on a particular subject is hazardous at best and leads to paranoia at worst. As words grow to sentences, sentences to paragraphs and paragraphs to pages, one becomes increasingly aware that what he is writing may not be read solely by "teenagers." Teachers, parents, lawyers and, yes, parents who are lawyers will have the opportunity to read and judge this work from their particular vantage points.

The facts are that as authors we can be neither teachers, parents nor lawyers and, thank goodness, we cannot be teenagers. We run afoul of the law's myriad exceptions, contradictions and geographic and governmental variations. If we become too specific as a lawyer or an educator, we are over the head of or simply confusing insofar as our intended audience is concerned. As to the professionals, teachers and lawyers, we become hopeless generalists restating common sense platitudes "everyone already knows."

Our purpose is to describe the law as it is. Constructive criticism and valid reform must be founded on a knowledge of the law as it exists today. I hope we are contributing to a foundation upon which to build.

Legal disputes are often settled between the parties. In the legal profession it is said that, if no one is entirely satisfied, you have probably reached a good compromise. I suspect that the same is true in a book of this sort. It has been a pleasure to be Albert Ayars' lawyer in writing this book. I will be forever grateful to him for giving me this opportunity.

John M. Ryan

CONTENTS

FOREWORD

The authors of this book have undertaken a commendable and difficult task. They have written a law book for secondary school students and their teachers, and have described laws and our legal system in understandable language. Such an effort is overdue.

One should not expect to become a lawyer by reading this small volume. Messrs. Ayars and Ryan have not attempted to take young readers beyond an acquaintanceship with laws that affect their lives and the system under which these laws are applied. Hopefully, this introductory acquaintanceship will prepare readers to participate in our system of government with a better understanding of law.

This book is timely. Many of the basic tenets of the legal profession, law schools and our institutions of government are being examined and questioned. If changes are made in laws, or the system that enacts and interprets laws, such changes should not alter the delicate balance between freedom and authority that sustains our democracy. Future voters should understand the necessity of maintaining a legal system that shields us from anarchy or tyranny.

The information available in this book is a needed supplement to traditional civics and government courses. It is important that students appreciate the rule of law in a free society.

William B. Spong, Jr.
Dean
Marshall-Wythe School of Law
College of William and Mary

THE TEENAGER AND
THE LAW

Chapter 1

WHY HAVE LAWS?

What is the law? Is it a cop? Is it a bald-headed detective on a TV show? Is it "the man," a hassle, a siren in the night or a long wait in a traffic court? What are laws and why do we have them? Why do we have people to enforce the laws, people to decide what the law is and lawyers who earn their living interpreting the law to others?

Someone once described the law as being represented by a single car stopped at a red light on an empty street at three o'clock in the morning. Why is this? Does that make sense to you? The purpose of this book is to try to explain the laws that apply to you, the American teenager. It is important at the outset to refer to the *American* teenager because others your age in many nations of the world do not have the same laws you do. In a majority of the countries of the world, people have little choice as to what the law is. They may care what the law is, but they lack power to use the law, to change the law or to benefit from the law's protection.

You are an American teenager and have many rights and responsibilities under the law. This is because you are free and, in a free society, the laws tend to be more complicated.

Wherever men have lived peacefully together, they have found a need to be governed by rules of conduct. These rules, or laws, state how we must behave toward our fellow man and toward the government that controls the civilization. They also protect our rights, often described as privileges. Governments may take many forms but, whether a country is governed by a king, a dictator or by the people themselves, as in America, a system of law controls the way the people will live together.

This book is about a democratic system of law, the law of the United States of America. Courses in history, government and civics provide a good background for understanding the type of government we have, how and why it began and the way in which it operates. This book will discuss the laws that are necessary to a democratic society. Why are they necessary?

Why Are Laws Necessary?

In order to live peacefully, people must feel safe with one another. Put another way, we want to own property such as a car, a farm, a fishing pole or money without fear of someone's taking it through robbery or violence. These are just some of our rights that the law protects. We all know that robberies occur, but we also can feel secure that our laws will punish those who commit robbery.

When we need property, such as a place to live and food to eat, we do not have to fight another person to obtain a roof over our heads, nor do we have to hunt game to put on our table. Our system of laws provides a peaceful means for us to earn money to buy food from someone who can safely stock and sell food as a business. The supermarket purchases its goods from farmers who are able to work peacefully on their farms. We may earn our living delivering the food the store-keeper sells and thus we see a chain of peaceful relationships that has been established under a system of law. Law in a democracy such as ours protects us by treating us equally and as individuals. Each citizen has an equal vote to secure representation in government. By the majority vote of individuals in support of a particular issue or a candidate, we control our law-makers and thus we make our own laws.

Why Do Laws Change?

The law is always changing. When our country was starting and natural resources were being discovered, laws were passed which protected ranchers and farmers and the people who mined precious metal. The U. S. Marshal, a colorful character on the TV screen, was in reality a true symbol of the law in the Old West. It was a serious matter when he strapped on his "peace maker" and strode bravely into the streets to capture a stagecoach robber. As our nation developed strength through industry, laws were developed which protected the worker and his union. The laws prohibited child labor and sweatshops. Today, as technology has come into our lives, our lawmakers have created various agencies to control scientific development. Examples of administrative agencies designed for this purpose are the Atomic Energy Commission, the Environmental Protection Agency and the Equal Employment Opportunities Commission.

Laws are created (passed or enacted), changed (amended) or eliminated (repealed) as the public becomes interested in special problems.

As our population grows to occupy all of the country's vast land area, a new pattern of lawmaking is concerned with our open space, our rivers and the natural resources which are being used up or polluted with increasing speed.

Laws are being passed which protect our air by setting standards for automobile exhaust systems, protect our waters by punishing those who spill oil and protect our land by regulating strip mining.

We have become aware that every person has the same rights under our laws as every other person. We have repealed laws requiring the payment of a poll tax in order to vote. We have passed laws requiring companies to hire all persons regardless of their race, sex, creed or the country from which they come. These are but a few examples of how our laws change to reflect what the public wants.

Not only does our system of laws change by the passage of new laws, but our existing laws "change" to the extent that they are enforced. The Supreme Court building in Washington, D. C., bears the legend over its entrance, "Equal Justice Under Law," reflecting a basic concept upon which this country was founded. Only in the past quarter century has the law which is the basis for this concept, our Constitution, been given true force and vigor. This emphasizes the point that our legal system is not just words on paper; our legal system reflects what the country's citizens want. By their vote, their voice and their action they give life and meaning to our legal system.

Why Understand the Law?

Why is an understanding of our legal system important to young persons even before they can vote?

You are a participant in our legal system. It is wise to prepare yourself to participate well. Laws and their administration affect our everyday lives, regardless of our age, although there are special laws that apply to the young. Let's take an example.

John Smith gets up each weekday morning at 6:30 a.m. because he has eighty-five papers to deliver before breakfast, and he has to be at school by 8:30 a.m. Since daylight saving time ended last month, it is not dark, but still he would like to get an extra hour's sleep. After the papers are delivered, John's sister, Mary, drives John and two other neighbors to school; all of them help pay for the gas. With the money John earns on his paper route, he hopes to buy a car next May when he is old enough to get a license. John's mother has agreed to sign the necessary papers, but he has to earn the down-payment and he will have to make monthly payments for the next two years. John's plans are somewhat in doubt because Mary received a ticket for speeding and, when she goes to court next week, she may lose her license. If she can no longer drive, John will have to walk to school, and that means John will have to get up an hour earlier. John isn't sure it's really worth it.

John's problem isn't very unusual. What may be surprising is the extent to which he is involved with different laws. You could probably list many laws that affect John. Here are examples:

1. John has to get up early on weekdays because a law provides that school will be taught Monday through Friday and, up to a certain age, John must go to school.

2. A law provides when it is 6:30 a.m. in the geographical zone in which John lives.

3. John has eighty-five papers to deliver because that is part of his contract with the newspaper. This does not involve a law except to the extent that laws provide for means to enforce contracts and specify whether John can even enter into a contract, since he is a minor.

4. A law provides for daylight saving time and states when it will begin and end.

5. Mary can drive because a law allows her to obtain a license. John cannot yet drive because the law sets an age requirement which he doesn't meet. Of course, the law sets a speed limit which Mary may have broken. The law has given a court the duty to enforce the laws to protect the public. In this connection, the court can punish people who drive too fast.

6. Mary has an agreement legally described as a contract whereby she drives her car, in return for which her passengers buy her gas. Although this is not a written contract, Mary can refuse to take a passenger if he or she "breaches" the agreement by refusing to pay for gas.

7. John cannot buy a car himself because a law says he is too young to sign a contract. His mother, an adult, can legally act on his behalf but, if John doesn't earn enough to make the payments, his mother can be sued and the car taken away. John cannot be sued.

8. The papers John's mother signed are regulated by laws. Among other things, they must state how much interest is to be paid.

9. The title to the car will be in a form required by law. It is the symbol of ownership and, by law, will be registered by the state. The car cannot be sold until a title is issued by the Division of Motor Vehicles.

These are only nine areas in which the Smith family is directly affected by the legal system we have created. You can be certain that there are many other laws that affect day-to-day life.

Since we have a great deal to do with our legal system, it is important to understand just what laws are and how they touch our lives and the world we live in.

Chapter 2

OUR LEGAL SYSTEM

How Did We Get Our Legal System?

A nation's legal system involves its laws and its courts. While our nation was colonized by people from many countries around the world, the legal system of most states is broadly based upon early law of England. The first colonies were English and their citizens were subjects of the English king. After the American Revolution, the original thirteen American states kept the English legal system, known as the "common law," changing it only to conform to our new democratic form of government. This system was carried westward to the Pacific and eventually became the basis for our state legal systems.

Several of our states were colonized by European countries other than England, and their legal traditions have roots in the continent of Europe. Texas, Florida and some Southwestern states still have laws which originated in Mexico and Spain. Louisiana never adopted the English system law and its laws are based on the French code of Napoleon.

What "Is" Our Legal System?

The basis of the English legal system, developed over the centuries, is known as common-law and it is a collection of

unwritten principles that came into existence as the result of
decisions made by the English courts and, earlier, the English
crown. It is a system based in many respects on rulings made
by judges and accepted by the English people as the laws that
governed their affairs. It must be understood that, even today,
not all of our laws are written.

As society became more complex, much of the common law
was "codified" or became written law, and our state and federal
codes trace their origin, in many instances, to ancient English
court rulings.

Who Makes Laws? Who Interprets Them?

Written laws, in many cases based upon our common law
heritage, are passed by the elected representatives of the people,
be they members of a City Council, a State Legislature or a
Congress. The court's duty is to interpret those laws as they
apply to an infinite number of factual situations. Very few law
cases are the same.

Court decisions which have interpreted the laws as they apply
to a particular factual situation are referred to in our legal
system as "precedent." Courts are usually ranked, beginning
with the lowest trial courts such as traffic courts, up to the
higher courts of appeals, the supreme courts of the various
states and the Supreme Court of the United States. A decision
of the higher courts sets precedent which the judges of the
lower courts will often follow in interpreting the same law.

What Is the Difference Between Civil and Criminal Law?

To gain a basic understanding of our legal system one must
be aware of the distinction between civil cases and criminal
cases.   Civil cases involve disputes between private persons.
They generally involve such things as contracts, property rights
or negligent conduct that results in injury to others. Criminal

cases always involve a government representing its citizens against an individual or group of individuals who are violating the government's criminal laws.

A third category of cases which falls under the general heading of civil cases is "equity." Equity cases are suits attempting to make a person do or stop doing a certain thing. This would include "injunctions" which, for instance, might order a person to stop obstructing his neighbor's driveway or otherwise stop him from doing some non-criminal act. Equity also includes domestic relations cases such as divorce, annulment and nonsupport. In discussing the difference between criminal and non-criminal laws, we refer often to the latter as "civil" law as it refers to the legal system historically based on the European continent. Let us first discuss the laws and then we will analyze our system of courts.

State Laws
How Do State and Local Laws Differ?

Starting with the county, town or city in which you live, there are ordinances passed or enacted by the community's governing body which are purely local in nature. These ordinances may prohibit swimming in a reservoir, provide for the admission price at a city zoo, set local speed limits or establish taxes or zoning laws within the city limits. Being local in nature, they cannot conflict with state laws.

Local ordinances cover matters within an individual community. State laws are designed to regulate the conduct of affairs and behavior on a statewide basis. For example, state codes contain a section defining criminal conduct; another section of the state law will specify how automobiles are to be sold, operated, inspected and licensed; other typical sections deal with hunting, banks, insurance and workman's compensation. The same laws will apply to every citizen in the state in the same manner.

It is in the state codes or "statutes" that we find most of our laws that pertain to the family; in particular, marriage, divorce, adoption and the rights and duties of parents and children.

A city law may, by local ordinance, establish a curfew requiring that all minors shall be home by a particular hour on weekday nights. This is a decision left in the hands of local government because local people know the nature of their city's problems. State law, however, will determine at what age a person is or is not a minor, and this age will be the same throughout the state and with regard to all state laws concerning minors.

This division between the local and state law enables a community to regulate its own local matters while providing a uniform system at the state level that applies to all citizens equally.

The Police and the Courts
Who Brings Cases to the Courts?

As we have stated at the outset of this chapter, courts are established to interpret the laws. In most states the local police are responsible for enforcing both city and state criminal laws. State police are generally responsible for law-enforcement problems outside local community boundaries, but they may be called into a particular locality to assist local police with severe criminal problems or public disturbances, such as riots, or natural disasters, such as floods or earthquakes.

The state courts administer the laws as they are brought before them, either by the police, in the case of criminal laws, or by its citizens, in the case of civil disputes. State agencies, sometimes called divisions or bureaus, have specialized law enforcement capabilities. In most states, there is an agency created to regulate the manufacture and sale of alcoholic beverages. The authority of a state alcohol control agency extends

state-wide. It would be particularly concerned with the sale of
alcohol to minors. This agency's enforcement powers would
include the power to revoke the liquor license of a restaurant or
a bar illegally serving under-age customers. Other agencies
might have special police powers in state parks or on state
waters.

State Courts

What cases do lower courts handle?

Generally the lowest rank of courts exists in each city, town
or county. These courts may be specialized to the extent that
one will handle only traffic cases, or petty crimes and misdemeanors; another will deal with civil cases concerning disputes
between local residents. In areas of low population density,
one lower court might handle all three types of cases, perhaps
scheduling traffic cases for one week in a month and criminal
and civil cases during other weeks.

In the lower courts, a person may, if he or she desires, go to
court without a lawyer. In traffic cases, as well as minor
criminal cases and civil suits, lawyers are not necessary, but it is
wise to discuss a case with an attorney before representing yourself. It is often said that the man who represents himself has a
fool for a client.

What other state courts are there?

A higher level of courts handles more serious cases as well as
appeals from the lower courts. These courts, often described as
courts of record, are the tribunals where most jury cases are
heard. The persons involved in the suit are always represented
by lawyers.

In almost every state, the courts above the courts of record
are limited to hearing appeals from the lower trial courts. These

are known as appellate courts. Some states have two levels of appellate courts, an intermediate appellate court and a single state Supreme Court. Others have only one appellate court, again a single panel of judges making up the state's highest court.

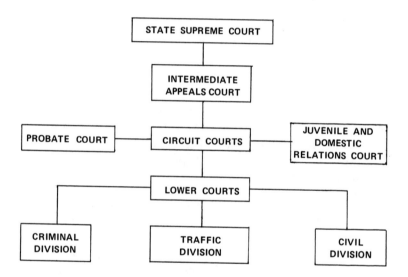

A TYPICAL STATE COURT SYSTEM

What is "jurisdiction?"

Most states have certain specialized courts which hear only certain types of cases. Juvenile courts fall in this category and will be covered separately in this book. Often there will be probate courts which only hear cases involving wills and inheritance problems. Almost every state has boards and commissions that act in the same manner as courts but hear only cases limited to such areas as public utilities, insurance or consumer affairs. In learning about courts, you should become familiar with the word "jurisdiction." This term refers to a court's authority to hear particular cases. Very often a court's name will give you an idea of the type of case it is permitted by law to hear. "Superior Court Criminal Division" pretty clearly says in its title that civil cases will not be considered in that particular court. Very often a court's jurisdiction may be limited even further.

Many lower courts can hear only those cases involving limited amounts of money and, if a case involves a claim for damages beyond that court's jurisdictional limit, the person will be required to bring his suit in a higher court. As we have seen, this may mean that parties in the case will be required to have a lawyer, so the difference can be very important.

Are laws different in different states?

We have been covering typical state legal systems. You must understand that every state has a different system. What you are familiar with in one part of our country may differ considerably from what you find when you move to another state. State laws often differ with regard to the age teenagers can be licensed to drive, own or inherit property, or be held liable for their negligent acts. These frequent differences between the laws of the various states have led to the rapid growth of another legal system altogether. This is a nationwide body of laws, courts and law enforcement officials that make up our federal legal system.

Federal Laws

Why have federal courts?

Americans move about their country with great ease and frequency. Many of us have lived in several states. Many people live in one state and go to school or work in another. Businesses often conduct their affairs in many states and, unfortunately, crimes very often involve the crossing of state boundaries.

Early in our history the federal system was established so that a citizen of one state could not take unfair advantage of a citizen of another state by hauling him into a local court likely to be partial to the local contestant. The familiar "home court advantage" may not have originated with the game of basketball, although such suspicions were more imagined than real. Also, as our nation grew, it became clear that there were areas of the law that should be the same for every citizen no matter where he lived.

Obviously, laws governing citizenship had to be the same throughout the nation. The means by which an immigrant became a naturalized United States citizen had to be the same in California as it was in New York. This is but one example of the need for a federal, uniform law.

As industry grew we learned that it was useless for one state to pass labor laws limiting the hours a child could be made to work when a sweatshop owner could simply move his business across a state line. The United States Congress, therefore, enacted child labor laws that protect children from oppressive working conditions in all states.

Which laws prevail in case of conflicting provisions?

Famous decisions of the United States Supreme Court

established long ago the principle that, where federal law covered a particular subject, state laws could neither change the federal law nor conflict with it.

As our country grew in size and complexity, more and more federal legislation was passed by the Congress. Industrial growth led to laws governing labor unions, corporate monopolies and the minimum wages. The expense of running our country led to federal income taxation and the growth of our transportation systems led to the establishment of federal laws that set transportation rates that would be fair for all Americans in every state.

These examples illustrate how federal laws arise from national problems and, as the country changes, so do the laws.

Federal Courts

What cases are tried in federal court?

The federal courts provide the system whereby cases involving our national laws are decided. There are federal courts in each state. Each federal court is governed by the same rules and has the same jurisdictional requirements.

Unless a particular federal law provides otherwise, the civil jurisdiction of the federal courts is limited primarily to suits involving more than $10,000 between citizens of different states. Lawsuits involving federal laws can only be heard by a federal judge or magistrate; in other cases which do not involve the interpretation of federal law, a person desiring to sue has a choice between the federal court and the state court. Under proper circumstances, a non-resident sued in a state court can "remove" or transfer his case from the state court to the federal court.

The structure of the federal court system itself is not complicated. At the lowest level is a magistrate who handles criminal misdemeanor cases and assists the District Court judge in certain civil matters. A person can be tried before a magistrate only with his consent, but there is no right to a jury.

What federal courts are there?

Above the magistrate is the United States District Court. This is the trial court of the federal system; in almost all civil and criminal cases one can have a jury as a matter of right. A party accused of a crime has an absolute right to an attorney whether he can afford one or not, although the right can be given up or "waived." In all civil cases, the parties to the suit must have lawyers. Appeals from cases decided in the District Courts are heard by the United States Circuit Courts of Appeal. There are eleven Circuit Courts, ten having jurisdiction over several adjoining states and one for the District of Columbia. Appeals from the decisions of the federal appellate courts are made to the Supreme Court of the United States. These appeals are not automatically granted except in certain cases. A party wishing to appeal to the Supreme Court must file an application stating his case in detail. Often a decision of the Supreme Court is necessary to settle legal questions that the Circuit Courts have disagreed on.

A decision of the United States Supreme Court is final. Only the Supreme Court itself can change its own interpretation of the country's laws. This it might do by "reversing" or changing a decision it made at an earlier time.

The United States Constitution

Must laws agree with the Constitution?

We have discussed local, state and federal laws and the courts that interpret our laws. Underlying this entire legal system is the United States Constitution. All laws must satisfy the requirements of our national Constitution. There are literally thousands of court decisions that have held laws invalid because they were unconstitutional and we cannot cover them in this book.

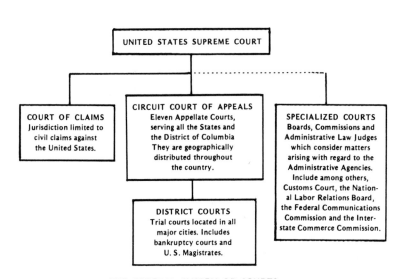

THE FEDERAL SYSTEM OF COURTS
The review of acting by the Specialized Courts depends on the Authority granted by Congress and differs from one Agency to another.

It is important to understand that all local, state and federal courts have the responsibility and the power to insure that citizens appearing in them are granted their constitutional rights. These rights are not limited to criminal cases but involve every aspect of our lives. They might insure, for instance, that a farmer's land cannot be taken for a new highway without a fair hearing. They guarantee that the government cannot control our free press and that all persons will have an equal right to a job regardless of their race, religion or sex.

Do citizens shape the legal system?

A democratic legal system depends upon the citizens it serves. They, as voters, elect their representatives who pass the laws. In many states they elect the judges. Without an understanding of the system, intelligent votes cannot be cast and our system is in danger. We must all realize therefore that we as citizens are the most important part of our legal system.

Judicial Selection

It is vital to our system of justice that only qualified men and women serve as the judges of the various courts. The manner in which judges are appointed or elected, the amount they are paid and the rules governing their conduct are under constant study. It is important that judges be impartial and free from outside influence. To assure that judges are qualified, lawyers' organizations frequently review the qualifications of persons proposed for judgeships and provide their recommendations to the state legislators. In the Federal systems, commissions have recently been established to examine individual qualifications. If a judge's conduct falls below certain standards, as recommended by the Canons of Judicial Conduct, a judge may be disciplined or even removed from his position. It is a credit to our system that such occurrences are rare.

Chapter 3

CITIZENSHIP AND LAW ENFORCEMENT

Citizenship

Citizenship means full membership in a country. The word "citizenship" comes from the Latin word "civitas," meaning a member of a city. Its meaning grew as the city-state concept of ancient times expanded to include our modern concept of country.

Our country offers its citizens protection when they are away from it and privileges at home. A country and its citizens are not really separate, for it wouldn't exist without them.

The citizens of a country guide its destiny. In our country, it is the faith and beliefs of the people that keep the spirit of liberty alive for the benefit of all citizens and aliens alike. Without this faith and these beliefs and without the support and observance of the laws by most of the citizens, the country, as we know it, would choke to its death on crime, litter congestion and greed.

Citizenship involves both *civic* rights such as the right to worship as one pleases, the right to freedom of expression, and the right to freedom of movement. It is our *civic duty* to support the government, obey its laws and defend it. Our *political rights* have some limitations (e.g., age, literacy, and residence). Typical political rights are the rights to vote and to seek election to office.

27

President John F. Kennedy advised citizens to "Ask not what your country can do for you. Ask what you can do for your country." Mr. Kennedy wisely understood that only by meeting our obligations as citizens could we continue to enjoy the privileges of citizenship. Democratic government fails unless citizens show the same eagerness to serve their country that they expect the country to show in serving them.

We all want to live happily and successfully. In order to guarantee these goals for ourselves, we must be sure that they are available to others as well.

Involvement Required

Who is obligated to prevent crime?

You have read or heard of incidents in which bystanders have witnessed crimes such as murder or burglary and didn't raise a hand or make a move to assist the victims or to bring the criminals to justice. This is contrary to the obligations of citizenship.

Laws reflect the will of the majority. Individual rights, freedoms and safety are dependent upon their being extended to all persons alike. The *prevention of crime* and the enforcement of the law are responsibilities of all citizens.

Persons who stand by and see others victimized by crime without attempting to help not only share the guilt but contribute to conditions through which they, themselves, can be similarly victimized.

How can we improve law enforcement?

We can improve law enforcement in our communities and in our country by doing everything we can to observe the laws and to see that they are observed by others. Our obligation along these lines includes:

Avoiding unjust criticism of the police;

Serving as a witness when called upon;

Reporting violations of the law;

Assisting the police and fellow citizens when threatened or attacked;

Accepting jury duty;

Understanding current problems affecting the community;

Participating in community meetings and improvement projects; and

Translating our beliefs into votes in every election—city, state, and national.

Obligations cited in the laws

How far do our rights as citizens extend? We have discussed the obligations required of citizens but of course we also enjoy rights unheard of in much of the world. Our freedoms, however, have limits, in particular when the rights of other citizens are affected. Let's look at some examples:

1. We are free to assemble and petition our government in opposition to or in support of its notices. We cannot, however, deprive others of their right to use the city streets and sidewalks. In gathering to protest or march for freedom, we cannot ignore the freedom of others; we must obey the laws by behaving peacefully.

2. We have the right to free speech but we cannot cry "fire" in a crowded auditorium when, in fact, there is no fire. To do so would endanger the safety of others. Laws punish those who make obscene or threatening telephone calls. Our rights to free speech cannot deny another person's right to be secure in his or her home or in public places.

3. We have the right to privacy, but that does not

extend to concealing criminal activity. The ancient English offense of "misprison of felony" is found in our Federal Criminal Code. It provides that anyone concealing and failing to report a crime may be fined or put in prison.

4. We have the right to bear arms. That is to own guns, but we cannot shoot them in populated areas. Certain guns such as short barrelled, "sawed-off" shotguns are prohibited. Further, we cannot carry concealed weapons without, in most states, a permit granted by the local government. As you can see, these gun laws are designed to prevent the use of guns for violent or criminal behavior and to protect the rights of fellow citizens.

These are but a few examples of how liberty is protected through limits on the freedoms we enjoy. Again, we all share these freedoms equally so we strive, as citizens, to observe their limitations and protect each other.

Is Civil Disobedience Justifiable?

Civil disobedience by an individual in the belief that a particular law is bad or unconstitutional and who chooses to violate it in order to bring a test case to the courts is a different matter. An individual may choose to disobey a law which he or she believes is unconstitutional. Such behavior challenges a particular law by bringing it to a court's attention and attempting to prove that it is contrary to the rights we have described. Such actions result in "test cases." Such persons don't encourage violence or mass civil disorder; they don't resist arrest and they're prepared to pay full legal penalties. They don't seek to violate the rights of others but rather they seek a chance to bring the matter to court to protect our rights as they believe them to be. In choosing this course of action, they show faith and respect for the law and the legal process.

An example of the individual test case approach is the action

of the Black student in the South who tried to enroll in a segregated (by state law) public school and who was refused but
persisted so that he could bring his case to court. The student
lost at first and appealed. The Supreme Court found segregated
schools violated the Constitution and declared that laws permitting segregation were invalid.

Public and Private Property

During the 1960's, acts of mob violence became quite common in this country. Some demonstration leaders tried to
justify the disruptions and their occupation of public buildings
and property. They attempted to distinguish between public
and private property and to claim a right to take over public
property. Whether a building or a school is public or private,
demonstrations and disorders interfere with the rights of others.
Such conduct ignores the rights of others and shows only dis-
respect for the law and legal process. The owners of public
buildings and streets have their rights as do the owners of
private buildings and private driveways. Other people's rights
are violated when public or private property is unlawfully taken
over. We cannot condone permitting the standards of a gang or
a mob to displace the standards of our society as set by law.
The violent capture of a school building is not civil disobedience; it is criminal conduct.

Student Voice in School Administration

Most modern school administrators believe in collaborative
(cooperative) planning and decision-making. That is, staff
members, students and parents all have an opportunity to contribute to the planning, implementation and evaluation of
school policies and practices.

However, it should be understood that, legally, students have
no right to make school rules or control school property.

Regardless of how much they are permitted to participate in setting curriculum, policies, rules of conduct and disciplinary procedures, the legal responsibility still lies with duly-constituted administrative authorities. Student participation in school government is a privilege granted to enable students to learn about making and enforcing laws—about self governance—by experience. It helps young people grow in leadership, responsibility and the motivation and initiative stimulated by having a voice in decision making. As students accept such responsibilities, they usually are given more. Responsible people are worthy of greater independence.

Summary

Good citizenship is practical citizenship. It requires us to be well-informed, open-minded and law-abiding people. Our rights as citizens are protected for our enjoyment only as long as the rights of our fellow citizens are protected. We must learn to balance our rights with our duties.

Chapter 4

MARRIAGE AND DIVORCE

Laws which concern the relationship of husband and wife, father and mother, and parent and child are found in every state code. Together they are known as the law of domestic relations and, as with so many areas of the law in our country, each state has its own particular differences.

Because we as a nation believe so strongly in the family and its importance to our country and society, our laws are designed to protect the institution. Our laws traditionally favor marriage. Even the income tax laws, in allowing deductions for dependents, encourage people to marry.

This is not to say that our laws make it easy for us to get married or divorced. If a marriage is to last and remain stable, it must be treated as a serious matter and not something we can "put on" or "take off" like an old coat. It can safely be said that marriages in most cases lead to children and, where possible, husband and wife should be encouraged to stay together as father and mother so that the children will have the full benefit of the traditional family upbringing. For these reasons, society frowns on divorce and, with the exception of very few states, our laws neither encourage nor make it easy to obtain a divorce.

When Can You Marry?

The minimum age at which you can legally marry varies from state to state. The most typical age at which a marriage license can be obtained without parent consent is 18, although, in some states, the age may be lower for girls. With parental consent, a marriage may be performed at an earlier age.

The "legality" of a marriage really refers to licensing requirements. You must obtain a license in order to be legally married. This means that certain physical tests must first be passed and that a license application be completed and a fee paid.

The official authorized to issue licenses must generally determine whether the persons who wish to marry are of the proper age and, if below the age of consent, whether they have obtained valid permission. He or she usually will request full names of the applicants, their places of birth and the names of their parents. He must be satisfied that both bride and groom are unmarried and that neither is under any "disability" such as mental illness.

The applicants for a marriage license are required to answer the clerk's questions under oath. In most states, giving false information is perjury and may be criminally punished. In many states it is also a crime, usually a misdemeanor, for a person authorized to issue licenses to do so without first making certain that the applicants meet the requirements of state law.

Individuals qualified to perform marriages are either court officials such as judges, magistrates or justices of the peace or they are priests, rabbis or ministers licensed by the state to legally marry persons who have obtained a marriage license. Often state law does not specify what the ceremony must be but requires only that both bride and groom freely and seriously express their consent to take each other as husband and wife. The consent must be given before a person licensed to perform marriages who then declares them to be married. Thereafter, the person who performs the marriage files a certificate with the court official who issued the license, stating that the marriage has taken place. Invariably, witnesses are required and their names will be recorded on the marriage certificate.

Most religions add significant ritual and vows to the marriage ceremony. These serve to impress the bride, the groom and the congregation with the important and sacred responsibilities that the marriage represents. Marriage laws usually recognize and permit exceptions to the basic state ceremony to accommodate different requirements of particular religions.

Marriage

Assuming that a valid marriage exists, what does it mean? Unfortunately, what marriage means is too often defined by what it isn't. Thus, we are familiar with divorce and the things that cause a marriage to break down. It is very hard to define what keeps it together. The law does not say what a marriage consists of, but it does define the relationship. In many ways this definition is reflected in the vows of the religious ceremony.

A marriage is a contract. Each party to a contract promises to do certain things and gives up his or her rights to do certain other things. You are "bound" to your spouse, owing him or her your loyalty. You leave all others, including your parents, and acknowledge responsibility to each other. A husband's obligations include working to support his family and providing the basic necessities of life. A wife, either through employment outside the family or in the home, may work also. Traditionally, a husband's activities are outside the home, in the world of business and labor, from which he gains the resources to support his family. A wife's activities are commonly performed within the home, where she uses these resources to create a successful, happy environment in which the family can grow.

In today's world, these traditional roles are frequently changed, depending on the ability and desires of the particular couple.   There is no law that says "a woman's place is in the home," or that a husband must be a "breadwinner."

To define marriage only as a contract may be a legal over-simplification.   Great writers, poets, philosophers, theologians, and judges have, at different times, described marriage as more than a contract, yet very few can agree on what that "more" consists of.   It is a personal relationship of extreme intimacy that defies a precise definition.   Partners in marriage make their relationship what it is.   Society encourages marriage because, over the centuries, it has proved to be an effective framework within which children may enter the world, gain experience, and eventually assume the responsibilities of adulthood.   It is not a perfect institution but, for the majority, it withstands day-to-day weaknesses, emotional letdowns, and physical ills to which we are subject.   It has been hailed as the bedrock of our national strength and character.

Viewing marriage as a contract or an agreement, we recognize it as having a positive existence.   It has limits or boundaries within which we do our best to stay.   To preserve a marriage we mutually sacrifice our purely selfish desires.   The law supports and strengthens the self-discipline that marriage requires.   One cannot simply walk away from a marriage and, for this reason alone, a couple may turn back and try again.

Marriages, in some instances, are quickly found to be defective.   If a marriage is entered into through mistake or illegally, the law provides for setting aside the relationship altogether, through annulment.   In other cases, despite all efforts to the contrary, an established marriage fails.   In such cases, the law permits the husband and wife to separate and, thereafter, independently lead their own lives.   This is made official by means of divorce.

Annulment

Occasionally, a marriage is performed that does not meet

the requirements of state law. Minors may misrepresent their age, or falsify their parents' consent or marry while under the influence of a drug. Such marriages are "voidable"; that is, they may be set aside or annulled through court action.

Annulment is a legal proceeding whereby a court declares that a marriage is void—that it never existed. There are, depending on the state, a number of "grounds" or reasons for annulment. If one or both of the persons married is under the age of consent, they, through their guardians (in some states referred to as their "next friend"), may institute legal proceedings asking to set aside the marriage. In many states, the suit may be filed by the minor's parent, as guardian, without the consent of the child. In deciding whether to grant an annulment in such cases, the court will consider the desires of the child.

Other grounds for annulment may include bigamy (one of the parties to the marriage is already married to another living person and has not been divorced), prior unknown conviction of a felony, fraud, impotency, or prior unknown prostitution. If a person is forced into marriage or goes through a ceremony as a joke, a marriage may be annuled. State laws prohibit marriages between closely related members of the same family, such as brothers and sisters or father and daughters. When such marriages occur, they also may be annuled.

Annulment proceedings must be brought without delay. Courts are reluctant to void a marriage if the relationship has resulted in changes in the persons' lives. If there is pregnancy or property ownership has changed, the court may deny a petition for annulment.

It may be difficult to understand how a court can say that persons who were married were in fact never married; that the marriage never existed. Remember that marriage is essentially a contract between two people, each agreeing to change his or her life in return for the other's agreement to the same effect. The court's action in granting an annulment declares that, because of fraud, mistake or illegality, no contract came into existence.

Divorce and Separation

While marriage is commonly thought of as a relationship closely tied to religion, divorce is not. There is no religious ceremony whereby a divorce is "performed." The legal proceeding by which marriage ends is not recognized by the Roman Catholic Church, and it is generally frowned upon by many other religions.

All states, however, permit divorce and have laws that specify the reasons or grounds for which a court will decree that a marriage is ended. Since marriage creates new property interests, divorce statutes contain provisions which permit marital property to be divided or "awarded" to one party or the other. Society's primary concern as to divorce is to be certain that minor children are provided with continuing support and guidance. For this reason, divorce laws make special reference to the custody and support of the children until they reach adulthood.

A divorce action, often called a bill or a complaint, is filed in a court having divorce jurisdiction. Every state has a requirement which specifies how long the party seeking the divorce must have resided in the state in order to obtain a divorce. Some states, particularly Nevada, have a very brief residence requirement; others may require as long as a year.

The suit must state a basis for asking for the divorce. Grounds for divorce include desertion, adultery, and cruelty in most states. Grounds for divorce in some states may be grounds for annulment in others. Thus, in some jurisdictions, when one party to a marriage has, prior to marriage, been convicted of a crime, the other person, if he or she did not know of the conviction, can sue for divorce. In some states, the same person could seek an annulment.

Some laws permit divorce if a married couple has separated and stayed apart for a long period of time, usually a year or more.

Frequently, the various grounds for divorce are divided into two categories. Certain more serious reasons such as physical cruelty or adultery will, if proven, entitle the suing party to an immediate divorce whereby the marriage is completely ended. Less serious grounds may result in a "limited" divorce, really a legal separation, by which the man and wife live apart in accordance with a court decree for a set period of time. The decree provides for the custody and support of any children as well as support for the wife if she is not self-supporting. If at the end of the time specified, usually a year, the couple does not reconcile, the legal separation becomes a final divorce.

When a divorce action is filed and comes to a court proceeding, testimony is often heard privately by a court official, sometimes known as a commissioner. Witnesses are normally required to support the testimony of the party seeking the divorce. The courts are diligent in seeing that the parties concerned recognize divorce as a serious matter, based on true marital difficulty, and not temporary unhappiness. If a court or marriage commissioner believes, from the evidence, that the parties have no real grounds, a divorce may be refused even though both parties consented and agreed to terminate their marriage.

When a married person goes to a lawyer seeking a divorce, it is the lawyer's obligation first to explore the possibility of reconciliation and, when reasonable, encourage the parties to go back together. The courts also inquire as to whether a couple's differences can be solved and the marriage saved.

If one partner does not want a divorce, the action can be "contested." In such cases, a full divorce hearing will be held. The spouse opposing the divorce will try to prove that the claimed grounds do not exist and will present evidence to that effect.

In other cases, each party may sue the other for divorce. A wife may claim desertion, in that her husband left their home. The husband may cross-claim that he is entitled to the divorce

because his wife forced him to leave by her cruelty or other behavior. In these unhappy circumstances, the court must decide
which, if either, spouse is in the right and grant the divorce
accordingly.

You may wonder why, if both the husband and wife claim
grounds for divorce, it makes any difference to whom the
divorce is given. The reason is that the divorce decree will
also dispose of the property owned by both husband and wife.
It may award alimony to the wife and, most important, it will
decide which parent will have custody of the couple's minor
children.

Alimony refers to money paid by a man to his former wife
for her support. The court, upon awarding the wife a divorce,
will have heard evidence as to how much money she needs for
her day-today expenses, shelter and food. The divorce decree,
based upon the judge's findings, will direct the husband to make
periodic payments until the wife dies or remarries. It may be
possible, in some cases, for the husband to make one large
lump-sum payment which, if invested, will return enough income to the wife to support her. In *some* instances, alimony is
paid by the woman to her former husband.

Property, such as land, a house, furniture and automobiles,
is frequently divided by agreement between the husband and
the wife obtaining a divorce. When they cannot agree, a court
will make the necessary decisions, perhaps ordering one to give
title to a house or automobile to the other, depending on
need and, in particular, the needs of the children.

A number of states, particularly in the West, have community
property laws. These laws state generally that any property
acquired by either husband or wife during marriage, and except
through gift or inheritance, belongs to both husband and wife.
Divorce proceedings in community property states may involve
a complicated analysis as to what is or is not community
property and, thereafter, a division of the property. In some
cases, it may be divided equally; in others, its division may turn

on which party the court feels is right or wrong and the circumstances of the case.

It is not uncommon, when an agreement cannot be reached, for the family home to be sold. This is not illogical since the divided family must have two "homes" and it is financially impossible to keep a house that is too large under the circumstances.

Custody of minor children, and particularly female children, is usually awarded to their mother unless she is unfit, unwilling or unable physically to bear the responsibility. Society has traditionally considered it a woman's obligation to raise young children, while a man's duty toward the family is to work outside the home to support his wife and children. This tradition is followed in custody proceedings even when it is the father who has sued and obtained the divorce.

The court's primary consideration is the welfare of the child and not the desires of the mother or father. The courts may, and frequently do, ask a child which parent he or she desires to live with. This is almost always done in private without either parent's being present. Whether the child's desires will be followed depends to a great extent on age and the judge's opinion as to the child's maturity. Most judges experienced in domestic relationships understand and appreciate the very difficult position of a child in such circumstances. A judge understands and accepts the very real possibility that a child often cannot make a choice between two parents, both of whom are loved, and will not force a decision.

It is important to understand that a divorce brings to an end the relationship of husband and wife and not the relationship of father, mother and child. A man may have failed as a husband and still be a good father. Unless the contact with a parent is judged to be harmful to the children, the courts will seldom prohibit a continuing parental relationship to the extent possible on the part of the parent not granted custody.

This is accomplished through visits and, in some cases,

divided custody. Frequently a divorce decree will set forth "visitation rights" which may provide, for example, that the children will spend two weeks each year with their father. It may specify that a child will spend alternate Christmas holidays in each parent's home. The courts believe that divided custody, each parent's having the children for a number of months, is generally unsatisfactory because of frequent changes in schools and living patterns.

Generally the divorce courts maintain continuing authority to decide custody questions. When a custodial award proves wrong, the court may change its decision and place children in the hands of the other parent or a grandparent if both parents prove unsatisfactory. This is a rare occurrence, however, and has been criticized as creating continual uncertainty and competition between parents for the child's favor.

There are situations in which a parent, denied custody, may try continually to contact the children and, in some rare instances, attempt to persuade them to leave or take them away involuntarily. In such cases, a court can issue an "injunction" ordering a parent to stop such activity. A failure to obey the court's order may lead to fines or imprisonment.

What Are the Actual Causes?

Because divorce is a national concern, efforts have been made to determine actual causes of divorce and, if possible, to take steps to reduce or eliminate them.

We mentioned earlier the most common legal grounds for divorce. Studies indicate that the most common actual causes resemble but do not duplicate the recognized grounds. Among the most common causes reported in the studies are mental cruelty, unfaithfulness, incompatability, lack of mutual interests, financial problems, disagreements over raising the children, relations with in-laws, general mismatching and lack of communication. Divorce occurs more often among the poor and uneducated and among those who rush into marriage. Marriages among teenagers and persons under 25 are, according to statistics, more likely to end in divorce than are marriages between people who marry at 25 and older.

Marriage is an important step in one's life. The decision should be made thoughtfully; yes, prayerfully.

Teenagers, in general, are serious, thoughtful people. They demonstrate great concern for others in many ways. They turn out en masse for March of Dimes Walk-a-Thons. They can be found in uniform performing volunteer nursing tasks. They visit old folks' homes, bearing homemade gifts and talking to and performing helpful tasks for lonely people. Many take heavy loads in school and still work half or full time after school. Such seriousness of purpose and dedication can be applied successfully to choosing a mate and making a marriage work.

Ferment among youth, the quest for equal treatment among the sexes, ventures into loose friendships or communal life, casual affairs and general permissiveness have affected the institution of marriage. As yet, however, it has remained our society's basic organizational structure for meaningful relationships and personal fulfillment. The family is likely to remain the bedrock of national strength and character. Its future role in our society will depend upon your generation and those succeeding it.

Our national divorce rate, 25 percent, is the highest in the world. This is regrettable indeed, for the failure of marriage often brings sadness and hardship to many people, most notably children. Our high divorce rate indicates that the marriage relationship is properly the subject of thoughtful reform. We have come to the realization that the status of women as full and equal partners to a marriage must be recognized. Women's rights to property and participation in marital decisions are subjects that our legal system must address. The serious realization of what marriage means and the importance of understanding its obligations as well as its joys cannot be overstated.

Chapter 5

FAMILY RELATIONSHIPS
AND THE LAW

The relationship between parents and their children is typically so informal and private that we don't often give much thought to the legal responsibilities that exist between them. Children in their adolescent years often question the limits that parents place on their activities and perhaps criticize parents for not allowing more freedom and financial support to their teenage desires.

Each state has laws which govern the relationship between parent and child. Our society believes that the family is the best means of preparing its young members for the responsibility of adulthood and citizenship and, therefore, by these laws, seeks to support and protect it. An understanding of the laws may help you understand your parents' attitude toward you.

The Responsibilities and Privileges of a Parent

Parents must control conduct

The law holds parents responsible for the activities, behavior and general conduct of their children. They are expected to know where their children are at all times, what they are doing and with whom. To accomplish this goal, parents often set hours at which children are to be in the house at night, and seek to know and approve of their after-school activities. They caution them against such dangers as hitchhiking or accepting rides and gifts from strangers. Local municipal laws support parents by establishing curfews and prohibiting hitchhiking and loitering around school grounds.

If parents are aware of and do nothing to prevent activity on the part of their child that may cause injury to others, they can be held legally responsible for such injury. As adults, they are expected to know that others might be hurt through such activity. If they do not take action to control their child's behavior and to prevent harm, they may have to pay for the damage the injured person suffered. This is true particularly when the parent's actions make the injury possible, such as instances in which a parent purchases fireworks for his child who, in turn, injures another through careless use.

Many states have laws making parents financially responsible for vandalism and damage to private or public property. If a parent actually encourages criminal conduct, there is little doubt that the parent will be held responsible as well as the child and may be punished by fines and perhaps imprisonment.

Food, Shelter and Care

Until their children mature or become self-supporting, parents are obligated to provide them with food, shelter, clothing and medical attention. Failure to support minor children is a crime in most jurisdictions. Child neglect (which may result in a child's being taken from its parents) can mean a failure to provide proper care or a failure to properly supervise and discipline children. A working mother must be certain that a responsible person is carrying out her responsibilities while she is away from the home. Parental neglect may result in the loss of custody when parents expose their children to immoral behavior or are habitual drunkards.

How Parents May Discipline Their Children

Reasonable rules

To meet these legal responsibilities, parents, in accord with the laws of the various states, may set any reasonable rules regarding behavior, dress and schedule of activities (such as bedtime or length and numbers of date nights). They may select whom their children may associate with, and they may prohibit association with others. They are free to set rules and demand obedience from their children. In this respect, "reason" is the key word; they may do anything within reason to raise their children in the manner they feel is desirable. They may impose physical punishment, such as spanking, or take other actions which cause discomfit, within reason, to the child. Punishment, of course, must not cause actual or permanent injury to the child and, in many states, there are child abuse laws which require doctors and teachers to report to the police cases which indicate that a child has been cruelly treated.

Education

As indicated in the "school" chapter of this book, parents share with the state (which is constitutionally responsible for providing education) the obligation for seeing that their children get an education. In this connection, parents are expected to see that their children attend school during compulsory school-age years, to control acts of truancy and to otherwise provide children with the proper necessities such as clothing and health care so that they may attend school.

The Children Have Responsibilities Too

Parents need your cooperation in carrying out their legal responsibilities. This includes obedience to reasonable rules and regulations, regular attendance at school and the performance of whatever reasonable chores your parents may require. In addition to jobs that you may have at your home, such as dishwashing or leaf-raking, you may earn money by delivering papers or babysitting. It may come as a surprise, but your parents are legally entitled to your service in or out of the house so long as they support you. Legally, your parents can claim your outside earnings and you do not have a legal right to claim payment of an "allowance" in return for your services. An allowance or payment for home jobs is a privilege, not a legal right. In most cases, parents wish to encourage their children to become self-supporting and do not wish to take their earnings.

Can You Sue Your Parents?

Lawsuits between family members have traditionally been discouraged as being harmful to a successful family relationship. Accordingly, many jurisdictions adhere to a "family immunity" doctrine based upon public policy to the effect that lawsuits between parent and child are contrary to the government's interest in preserving family unity and discipline. This doctrine applies primarily in the field of civil negligence actions in which a parent or a child is injured by the other through carelessness.

Some jurisdictions have eliminated the doctrine altogether, permitting children to sue their parents. Others have drawn a distinction based upon whether the parent was engaged in parental duties at the time the injury occurred.

If the child is "emancipated," that is, self-supporting, the courts are more inclined to permit parent-child litigation.

Lawsuits between parent and child which concern the ownership of property, particularly when it is transferred by will or by a state inheritance law, are infrequent but not unusual. It may be necessary to bring legal action to clear up any doubts as to the title to land, and the best way to accomplish this is by obtaining the opinion of a court.

When Are You in Full Charge?

The doctrine of "emancipation" is important to young people. Emancipation is unique in our system of laws because it originates not from the traditional common law of England but from ancient Roman law. When a minor child reaches the age of adulthood, we can say that he or she is automatically, "by operation of law," emancipated; that is, free to control his or her own life. The term, however, is most commonly used to describe the process whereby parents release a minor child from their custody or control before adulthood.

In many states, the steps necessary to accomplish emancipation are provided by statute. Where this is not the case, no formal procedure is required and emancipation is accomplished simply by the parents' action in freeing the child to care for himself or herself. A court-appointed guardian cannot emancipate his ward. A court must act to terminate such a relationship.

Assuming that parents decide to completely emancipate a child, what are the results of this decision? Basically, the doctrine applies only to the parent-child relationship. The rights and responsibilities related to custody and control are ended. An emancipated child's earnings are his own, and his parents' obligation to support terminates.

The state government does not give up its right to control the activities of its young citizens, and laws relating to minors still apply after emancipation. When an emancipated minor sues or is sued, a guardian will be necessary. Statutory age requirements in regard to employment, voting, driving and marriage are still applicable to the emancipated child in most states.

You will learn that a minor is limited in his ability to enter into contracts and may not be held responsible for contracts he does sign. The exception to this rule is that a minor may still be held liable on contracts for "necessaries." This term refers to the basic necessities of life such as food or shelter. An unemancipated child is usually provided such things by his or her parents. With the exception of agreements to pay for necessaries, there are few contracts for which the unemancipated minor child can be held responsible.

In the case of an emancipated child, the responsibility for necessaries is his own and he may be held liable on a broader range of contracts. This is not to say that the local clothing store will be any less reluctant to open a charge account in the child's name.

Because the means by which parents may emancipate a child vary widely, the courts have interpreted the process in differing ways. It is fairly well settled that emancipation may be limited in scope by the parents, may be for a shorter period than the time remaining for the child to reach adulthood, and may be terminated or revoked by the parent.

The law does apply to the family even though we don't often sense its effect. In fact, insofar as the family is concerned, the law is only a silent partner. It is only when the family relationship is threatened by misconduct, or by the failure of a family member to observe his or her obligations, that the law speaks up. We should always remember that it's there if it's needed.

Adoption

State laws provide for adoption. Through this process, the children of parents who are, for various reasons, unable to raise their children are taken into and become a part of another family. The procedure by which this takes place is carefully overseen by the courts to be certain that the best interests of the children are protected.

To avoid distress in later life, the statutes governing adoption generally provide for a complete termination of the original, natural parent-child relationship, and a full acceptance on the part of the new or "adoptive" parents of all responsibilities toward the child. The child owes all the duties of a natural child to his or her "new" parents and is subject to their control.

An adopted child is given the family name of his adopted parents and they are under obligation to support, educate and care for the child until adulthood is reached. The adoptive parents have full rights to custody of the child as against those of the natural parent or parents and, except in very rare circumstances, the child may not be returned to his or her original parents. By the laws of most states, adopted children acquire the same status as the natural children of the adoptive parents for the purposes of inheritance.

Not infrequently, adopted children want to learn the names of their real parents. In the past, it was thought that such information would be harmful to the new relationship, and records were either not kept or were maintained in strict confidentiality. Today, the public's attitude has changed to a degree, and reforms are being considered which will enable adopted children to learn more about their origins.

Chapter 6

THE FAMILY AND THE STATE

Why Is the Family a Government?

To understand the law as it affects young people, one can't overlook the relationship between our government and the family. Traditionally society has considered the family as a "government" in itself. By this we mean that the family manages its own internal affairs. Typically the parents exercise strong disciplinary authority when their children are very young. This gradually declines as the children grow older and, eventually, they gain complete independence.

How Do Laws Control Family Affairs?

The state is directly concerned, however, with the family's activities outside the household. Through legislation, our state governments regulate children's education, employment and working conditions. They determine when the individual can vote, drive, drink alcoholic beverages and generally conduct his or her affairs in the world outside the family.

The state and local governments are directly concerned with criminal or delinquent conduct. When a child commits a crime, the state law enforcement authorities and juvenile courts, and not the parents, have the duty, in the public's interest, to apprehend and punish the juvenile offender.

When the family is weakened or breaks apart as in the case of divorce or death, state legislation plays a vital role in protecting the interests of minor children. In cases of divorce, the state courts award custody of minor children to one parent or the other in accord with the best interests of the child. When neither parent is fit or able to keep and properly raise an infant, state legislation provides the means whereby a legal guardian can be appointed. The guardian, once appointed, has legal custody of his "ward" and has the responsibility for taking care of and protecting any property the child may own. In many states, a child above a certain age, usually between fourteen and sixteen, has the right to express a preference or "nominate" who his or her guardian shall be. This nomination is subject to court approval and may be challenged by relatives of the child. In the case of very young children, a family, unrelated to the children, can, through adoption, become the legal parents.

The state's role as a protector of minor children is based upon the old common law doctrine of "parens patriae" which referred to the king and meant "father of his country." In our democratic system, the state, in many instances, fulfills the role of parent to its young citizens who, because of their age, are not considered able to protect themselves.

The state is, in effect, a third parent of children whose parents, either together or apart, are unable to care for a child or are unwilling to agree as to its care. As mentioned in the following chapters, the state, through its court system, actively engages itself in protecting children who are injured or who injure others, who enter into business transactions, who inherit property or whose parents are unable or unwilling to properly care, educate and provide medical treatment for them.

When Does a Parent Lose Custody of a Child?

The right of parents to the custody of their children is considered basic to our democratic society. Rights, however, carry responsibilities and, when the courts find that those responsibilities have not been met, they have the equitable power to act promptly in the child's behalf. Such action may take the form of supervision in the case of a child who cannot be controlled by his parents. In these instances, the child is often made subject to the control of juvenile probation authorities in addition to his or her parents' control. The state may protect a child temporarily by appointing a guardian to be responsible for defending his or her interests in a lawsuit or it may take complete custody of the child in situations in which parents prove unfit or the child behaves criminally.

Cases involving the custody and control of children are often charged with emotion. The parents' and the child's constitutional rights to due process, fair trial and legal representation must always be protected, and it is the court's constant obligation to see that this is done. When a guardian is appointed to protect a child's interest, such guardian is charged with the responsibility of assuring that the child's personal rights and property rights are not violated. A guardian will usually be required to take an oath to that effect and to post a bond when property rights are involved.

A bond is, in effect, an insurance policy in a set amount of money. It stands as security against the possibility that a guardian might fail in his or her responsibilities. Should this happen, the bond serves to pay the minor for any losses suffered as a result of a guardian's mistakes.

Chapter 7

CIVIL LAW – CONTRACTS

Three Areas of Civil Law

In the first chapter we stressed the role of law in regulating relationships among people. We have pointed out the distinction between criminal and non-criminal laws. As we use the term civil law in this chapter, we refer to those laws that do not concern crime. The term can, as mentioned before, allude to the legal systems of Europe; but that is not our usage here.

The civil laws we are concerned with are those which deal with our day-to-day lives. These are the laws about such things as the purchase of a house or a car, buying a dress, renting an apartment or receiving injuries in an automobile accident.

Since Americans are engaged in many activities, there are many, many categories of civil laws. Crimes and criminal cases receive considerable attention in the daily news columns, but, in reality, criminal problems occupy a rather small portion of our legal system's activities.

Civil laws may be broadly divided into three major areas; they are *contracts, property* and *torts*. The law of contracts concerns agreements between people which create binding obligations on the contracting parties. When a contract is broken, the law says it is "breached," and our legal system provides a remedy for the breach of a contract by either award-ing money to the innocent party or by making the non-innocent party perform his or her obligations. Property law concerns the ownership, use and transfer of a thing of value whether it be a farm, a boat or a book.

The word "tort" comes from the Latin word for "twisted." Indeed, the law of torts twists its way through every aspect of our lives in such a way as to make it almost impossible to de-fine. A close but not an exact way to define it would be to say that a tort is a non-criminal wrong for which the law pro-vides a remedy.

Torts usually involve negligent or careless conduct which hurts others. Most cases involving automobile accidents can be described as tort cases. In such a situation, a court will be asked to make a careless driver pay money to the non-careless driver to compensate the latter for bodily injuries and damage to his automobile.

There are many other categories of civil laws which are close-ly related to the three broad categories we have described above. The law of damages, for instance, is applied in cases involving contracts, property and torts to determine how to compensate a person whose contract has been breached; who has incurred a property damage; or who has been injured in an accident. The law of evidence concerns the proof provided to support a damage claim and will be applied in trials arising under any of the three areas. The law of damages requires that the person seeking recovery present specific proof as to the amount of his/her loss. The law of evidence requires, in each type of dispute, that the proof be trustworthy. For that reason, hearsay evi-dence is usually not accepted.

There are also other separate fields of law that may not directly relate to either contracts, property or tort law. Ex-amples are taxation, divorce and civil rights. It is seldom that a case arises, however, that does not in some way concern these three bedrock areas.

Civil laws, and particularly the three areas (contracts, property, torts) described above, directly affect minors and their rights and responsibilities. Your ability to make contracts; to own and use property and your rights and responsibilities when you are injured or injure others are of great importance both to you as a minor and to the society in which you live. Let us take a closer look at how the civil laws affect young people.

Contracts

In many respects the contract is the heart of our legal tradition. In theory the contractual relationship is central to our government in the sense that, in return for the government's protecting our lives, families and possessions, we owe our government our loyalty. In schools across the country, the day begins with a pledge of allegiance to our country's flag, and this reflects our obligation to our country.

Indeed, of the three basic areas of our legal system—contracts, property and torts—the first is dominant and is involved in the other two. We shall see that we buy land or real estate by using a contract known as a deed which is the symbol of real estate ownership. In tort law, the concept that a negligent person must pay for the injury he causes implies an obligation of each of us to behave with care toward all others. When we breach that obligation, a jury may decide we must pay for our mistake.

Basic Essentials of a Contract

A contract is an exchange of promises; for example, a mechanic promises to repair your car in return for which you promise to pay him. There is an infinite variety of contracts covering any number of transactions, but there are certain basic concepts that apply to every one. There must be two or more parties. A "party" can be a person, a company, a government; almost any entity that is legally able to enter into an agreement. All parties to a contract must agree. Each party must receive what in law is known as "consideration" for his, her or its promise; this means that each party must receive some benefit. In the car repair illustration above, the money paid the mechanic is his consideration; the repairs are the car owner's consideration.

Each party must understand the terms of the contract and mean to be bound by them. If John offers to repair Fred's car, he must mean that, if Fred accepts his offer, he will do what he offered to do. If Fred accepts John's offer, he must mean that he will pay the amount John offered to do the work for.

In addition, the contract must meet the requirements of any laws that apply to it and it cannot be for an illegal purpose.

The above paragraphs cover the basic essentials of a contract. Other considerations may determine whether a contract is made but, if the essentials are not present, then there is no contract. What would happen in such a case? It could mean simply that none of the persons involved has to do what he said he would do, since there is no contract. If Fred tells John, "I'll pay you that $10.00 I owe you if you'll repair my car," there is no contract. Why?

When two or more persons enter into a contract and one fails to keep his promise, the other can file a lawsuit seeking damages for breach of contract. If the essential requirements for a contract are absent, a lawsuit seeking damages for non-performance would fail because there is no contract to breach.

What was believed to be a contract is described in such situations as void and unenforceable. A person suing in such instances cannot recover damages for breach nor can he expect a court to make the other party do what was supposed to be his obligation.

In some cases, a contract that has come into being is "voidable." This means that, in such cases, even though the essentials were present, one of the parties can refuse to perform his obligation without being responsible for harm to the other party. This has particular importance in this book because this is true of minors, as mentioned in Chapter 5.

A person who is, by state law, a minor can "avoid" a contract if he or she so desires before becoming an adult. This means that, as a general rule, a minor can refuse to perform his or her end of a bargain on the grounds that he or she is too young to make a contract. The option to avoid a contract belongs to the minor; that is to say that, once a contract is made, only the minor can refuse to perform, not the other party unless he or she too is a minor.

It should be said that this general rule "cuts" both ways. In many jurisdictions, the rule is interpreted to mean that a minor cannot make a contract and many businesses, particularly automobile dealers, simply refuse to sell directly to a minor. This is why, in so many cases, a car must be purchased and financed in a parent's name even though the young person has earned and paid "consideration" to the dealer.

Also, if the minor decides to "avoid" his contract, he may have to return any consideration he received under the terms of the contract.

Once a minor who has entered into a contract becomes an adult (described in many situations as having reached "majority"), he can "ratify" or accept its benefits and responsibilities, or he can disaffirm or "repudiate" the contract and be free of any responsibilities. It is a general rule that a contract that was completed while one is a minor will be considered valid when he or she reaches majority unless some step is taken to repudiate it. A contract that is still in the process of being performed, such as an apartment rental agreement, is invalid unless some step is taken to ratify it. It should be understood that ratification or repudiation can be done by an act other than an outright declaration one way or the other. Thus an infant's lease of an apartment may be ratified if, after becoming an adult, he continues to live in the apartment; and, as a tenant, he will have to pay the rent.

Almost all of the foregoing is subject to variations from one state to another. Because of these variations between jurisdictions, we must often refer to the "general rule" as to particular situations. In the same sense, there are certain exceptions to the laws of contracts as they apply to minors.

A minor may be unable to completely avoid a contract under which he or she receives things that are basic necessities such as food, medical care or education. The thing contracted for must be truly necessary and not a luxury, and it must be for his or her personal benefit and not for his or her family, friends or his business. In such cases, a court will enforce a minor's contract to the extent that he will have to pay the reasonable value of the necessity he obtained. Neither money nor an automobile is considered a basic necessity!!

A minor cannot avoid a contract imposed by law. If, in the case of a divorce, a minor enters into a separation agreement requiring the support of infant children in his ex-wife's custody, he cannot avoid such a contractual obligation since the law requires it.

Chapter 8

CIVIL LAW — AND PROPERTY

The second broad field of civil law concerns property. We usually think of property as consisting of land or possessions. This last word comes closest to the legal notion of property since property law is concerned not so much with *what* we possess as *how* we possess it.

When we ask a friend whether he has any property, we are really asking him whether he has the right of control over anything. If the reply to our question is, "Yes, I have a record collection," we are being told by our friend that he has certain rights over his collection. He has the right to sell his records or trade them; he has the right to give them away or even to throw them away. The law protects these rights.

Property Interests

The word "interest" is often used in describing a person's rights over property. If two or more persons own a piece of property together, they may be said to have a "joint" interest. A lender such as a bank may require the right to sell the borrower's property if his loan is not paid back. The property is security for the loan and the bank is said to have a "security interest" in the particular property. If we have borrowed money from the bank to buy a car, the bank's security interest will limit our ownership interest. If we are unable to repay the bank, it may "repossess" our car and sell it in order to get back its money.

An owner of property may limit his own interest by renting his property. Once an apartment is rented, the landlord, for the term of the lease, loses his right to possession. A landowner may allow a farmer to grow crops or permit a gravel company to operate a quarry on his property. In each case a different interest exists which the law regulates through our old friend, the contract.

The Public Interest in Property

Even if one's ownership interest in a piece of property is complete (that is, no other person has any rights over the property), that ownership may be ended in the "public" interest. Thus, it may be in the public interest for a state highway department to take your property for a new highway. The state would pay you a fair price for your land with money collected as taxes from the public. In such a case, the government represents the public interest and the process by which it so acts is known as the power of "eminent domain."

The use of your property may be limited by the government so as to protect your neighbors' property rights. Through "zoning regulations," one is often restricted as to the type of building that can be erected in a particular neighborhood. The city's "building code" will specify the basic requirements that each building must meet to protect the public's health and safety. A zoning regulation may prohibit your building a factory in a residential neighborhood; a building code provision may require you to have a fire escape.

It is certainly in the public interest that you do nothing illegal on your property. State and federal antipollution laws may prohibit a landowner from releasing dangerous fumes or smoke into the air or from polluting nearby streams. The criminal codes will prohibit your growing marijuana in your backyard.

Two Kinds of Property

Property usually is divided into two broad categories. The term "real property" refers to land or real estate and the permanent structures "attached" to the land such as a house or a barn. All other property is known as "personal property."

The definitions of real and personal property seem easy to understand but, in practice, they can become very complicated. With land, one person or a company could own the land below the surface, as in the case of mining or oil rights, while another could own the surface itself. Timber and crops growing on land are considered real property but, once cut or harvested, they become personal property. The varieties of real property interests are many, and they are far too complex to cover here.

Personal property can consist of "tangibles"; that is, things we can move, see and touch, such as a book or a sailboat. It can also be "intangibles" which cannot be held in your hand or, in some cases, even seen. Intangible personal property might be a debt or a right to sue. If Robert owes Ned ten dollars, Ned has a right to collect that money. If Ned, in turn, owes Mary ten dollars, he might give his rights against Robert to Mary in payment. The debt is property, intangible property, which can be controlled by its owner.

Personal property can consist of many things. An author's creation such as a book, a play or a song is property, and the law will protect ownership through copyright laws. Money is personal property as are stocks and bonds. Since debts are personal property, the bills due a store from its customers, known as "accounts receivable," can be given as security for a loan at a bank or given to another company in payment of a debt.

You may ask, why is there a distinction made between real and personal property? How does it affect me? The answer is that the law treats each class of property differently. Since real property is immovable and, to a large extent, is indestructible, ownership in some form essentially continues forever. Therefore, its transfer within a family or from one person to another is subject to different legal requirements than the transfer of personal property.

Personal property, broadly speaking, loses value as it ages. It is easily and frequently bought and sold and, in many cases, changes as it is used in making other things.

Personal property is usually made or created by its original owner. Typically, it changes or is used up and ceases to exist in its original form. Land, or real property, with some exceptions, is not made. Historically, land is the source of our most vital personal property, food, and as such it has long meant power and a source of wealth to kings and countries. Because of these important distinctions, the laws regarding the ownership of real property are more complex. It is important to know who the previous owners were in order to be certain that the "title" to the land is clear of defects. Can you imagine building a house on a piece of property that you are not sure you own? In such a case, does it make much difference who owns the lumber or bricks your builder uses to build your house?

If you own a piece of land, your ownership is called a "title." The title is represented by a written document known as a "deed." A deed is actually a contract of sale signed by the seller of the land and which transfers ownership or "title" to the purchaser. The deed describes the land and states the terms upon which the land is sold. It also describes what the seller's interest is in the property and may or may not make certain guarantees that the seller's title is a good one.

A complex system designed to record the ownership of land is maintained in every state. Before buying a piece of land, the purchaser will invariably go to the city or county clerk's office, the registrar of deeds or a similar office and thoroughly "search" the "chain of title" to be certain that the seller's title is a good one. Once the purchaser of land is certain the title is clear, he will complete his purchase and, in turn, record his deed so that his title is made a public record. No such elaborate system exists as to personal property.

Public and Private Property

From the standpoint of ownership, property may be divided into two other categories, public and private. What we have discussed to this point in terms of real and personal property refers primarily to private ownership. There is property, however, that belongs to all of us and to which no one has individual rights. Public property is maintained for us by our city, state and federal governments with money we pay in the form of taxes. It may include a national park, an historical landmark or an interstate highway. Our rights as citizens to enjoy public property are protected. It may be rented to private individuals, but it cannot be sold to them.

Do Minors Have Property Rights?

Our discussion has served only to introduce the reader to the subject of property law. This is necessary to understand a minor's rights insofar as property is concerned.

Earnings and Personal Property

How a child acquires property is important in determining whether he owns it. The traditional rule is that a parent has an absolute right to his child's earnings. Although seldom the practice in most households, a parent may demand and receive from his child money earned babysitting, delivering papers or washing cars. When a child is injured and the family goes to court, the child's parents have a right to recover money their child might have earned had he not been injured.

In most cases a minor's earnings are not large, but what about a young actor or musician? Earnings in some cases might be substantial.

The rule that a child's earnings belong to his parents is subject to several important qualifications. The common law reason behind a parent's right to a minor's earnings is that, in return for such earnings, the parents are obliged to care for their child. If the parents do not do so, they are not entitled to anything.

Property of any kind received by a child other than in the form of earnings belongs to him absolutely. If a grandparent gives a minor furniture or if a child inherits land, wins a bicycle or receives the proceeds of an insurance policy, in each case the property is his. This general rule is qualified in many jurisdictions to the extent that parents are by law charged with the care and management of their children's property. This requires them to take care of their children's assets and they can, therefore, decide how the property is to be used. They may not sell or use a child's property for their own purposes.

When a minor acquires property of substantial value, the court will frequently appoint a legal guardian to protect and preserve the property until its owner reaches adulthood. In many jurisdictions, a child's "natural" guardians, his parents, are usually chosen, but other courts and some state laws express a preference for an independent guardian. The guardian will be required to report periodically to the court as to the status of his "ward's" property.

Inheritance

In most cases, the ownership of property changes at the time of a person's death. The process is both involuntary and inevitable; you can't take it with you, and ownership must pass to someone else. A person who receives property when a relative dies is said to "inherit" the property and is known as an "heir." Since many young people acquire property through inheritance, it is important to know how our laws provide for the change in ownership that occurs when a property owner dies.

Learning some basic terms may be helpful. The real and personal property that a person owns during his life is known as his "estate." While this does not mean only one's possessions at death, it is at that time that the extent of one's estate becomes final. The field of law concerning the transfer of property at death is popularly known as "estate law."

Wills

A "will" is an important legal document whereby a person can choose who is to receive his property once he is gone. A personal representative or executor, approved by a court, has the responsibility of determining what the estate consists of and distributing it as directed by the will. If there is no will, the property will be distributed as provided by state law. A person can write a will by himself without a lawyer's advice, but there are many technicalities in the law that must be satisfied. If the will is not properly written, it will be ignored and property will be distributed by state law.

The disadvantages in obtaining a will are, first, its cost, since one should hire a lawyer and, second, the simple passage of time. Early in life you may wish to leave certain property to certain people; later in life you may change your mind and, therefore, you will have to change your will.

There are far more advantages than disadvantages in having a will. Since the state and federal governments tax property or the transfer of property at death, a will may be written so as to reduce taxes and, therefore, increase the amount the heirs will receive. As we have said, when no will exists, state law will apply; and this could mean that some persons will receive property who the deceased did not intend to receive it or who do not need it as badly as others.

A will makes it unnecessary for those who survive you to decide questions about your property. Usually legal expenses are lower when there is a will. Frequently, if an estate must be divided among a number of relatives, the personal representative must sell property and divide up the cash proceeds. This is unfortunate if the property in question has a "special" value as do antiques, jewelry or an old family home. With a will, such things can be given to those relatives who will value and care for them.

State laws which specify who is to receive the property of a person who dies without a will are generally known as laws of "descent and distribution." Generally, the surviving husband or wife, if the deceased was married, receives one-third of the estate and the children receive two-thirds. If there is no living husband or wife, then the children may receive the entire estate. If there are no children but there is a surviving husband or wife, then he or she may have to divide the property equally with the brothers or sisters of the deceased. From this point on, the property may be divided among parents, grandparents, aunts, uncles and cousins. Think of the confusion and legal expense a will might avoid.

Most modern state laws provide that adopted children can inherit in the same manner as natural children. The child of a parent who has remarried inherits from his stepparent in the same way as would a child of both. The children of unmarried parents, in a number of states, may be able to inherit only from their mother. Again, if there is no will or the will is defective, the state law will be strictly applied without any consideration of the hardships that might arise.

The Guardian

Will or no will, it is the court's responsibility to be certain that a minor child's property is protected until he or she reaches adulthood. Unless the property left to a minor has little value, the court must appoint a "guardian" to serve this purpose. Many states provide that parents can, in their will, select the person whom they wish to be their child's guardian. A guardian is responsible to the court to protect the child's property and provide for care and education of the child.

A guardian is responsible and has general authority to care for the day-to-day welfare of the child. If the child owns property, the guardian is required to keep it separate from his own and inform the court each year as to how the child's property has been cared for.

It may be necessary for a guardian to sell a child's assets and, in such cases, court approval is usually required. Courts are reluctant to agree to the sale of assets unless money is needed for the child's welfare.

We have learned that, before a person becomes an adult, his or her property is controlled by others. The minor's parents, a custodian, or a legal guardian appointed by a court have control over the use of the property. They must always act in the best interests of the minor.

Adulthood

How does the minor gain control over his or her property on reaching adulthood? The guardian, at that time, no longer has any control over the property and must give to the new adult the property and any documents representing ownership.

If a minor owns real estate, the deed to the property is already in the name of the child, and his guardian simply gives him the deed when he reaches adulthood. A legal guardian who is responsible for taking care of property must account for money he receives such as rent or dividends. A court or an official appointed by the court must approve the guardian's accounts before he or she is released from guardianship obligations.

Also, the guardian must wind up his affairs with his ex-ward, and this settlement would include such steps as delivering keys to property, signing such documents as may be necessary to transfer accounts, and fully informing the former minor as to the nature, status and whereabouts of all of his or her property.

Much has been said about guardians and the responsibilities of the states through the courts to be sure that a minor's property is protected. Often such property is of modest value, consisting of a savings bond, a share or two of stock, or the proceeds of a small insurance policy. In such cases, the court appointment of a guardian may not be necessary. A lawyer or the Clerk of the local court should be consulted to determine whether a guardian is required by state law.

You have seen that the law on property is complex. Our laws are designed to protect a minor's property until he or she can assume that responsibility. The state, through its court system and a system of guardians, oversees its obligation to protect that property.

Chapter 9

CIVIL LAW — TORTS

Generally, minors can be held responsible for careless acts that harm others. Such acts are called "torts." If a child riding his bicycle on a crowded sidewalk fails to look where he is going and knocks another person down, causing injury, there may well be grounds for a suit against him for the damages arising out of the injury.

In many states there are limits on this general rule. Thus it is frequently the case that a child under seven years of age will be considered too young to be negligent. In effect, the law says that, at or below a specific age, the child simply does not have sufficient experience, understanding or education to foresee the potential harm he could cause.

In the law of torts, foreseeability is a central question. The jury will be asked to decide whether the person being sued for damages knew or reasonably should have known that his actions would hurt the injured person. We can see that a six-year-old probably would not fully understand how his bicycle might cause harm to another person.

Typically, children between the ages of seven and the early teens, usually fourteen, may be held liable for their actions. The law still gives them the benefit of the doubt; they are presumed to be incapable of negligence, but this presumption can be "rebutted." This means that a child between seven and

fourteen is presumed to be unable to appreciate the probable
result of his careless act.   The injured party suing him can
overcome this presumption by presenting evidence to the
contrary.

Beyond the age of approximately fourteen, a minor's conduct
will usually be judged by the same standards as an adult's behavior.   Plainly stated, the laws reflect that one's sense of
responsibility develops as one grows older and, therefore, his
or her behavior toward others must also become more and more
responsible.

Negligence is the most frequently used term in the field of
tort laws; it can mean many things. A person can be negligent
without ever seeing the person he injures as when a restaurant
owner allows food to spoil and a patron later becomes ill. A
person can be directly negligent by driving through a red light,
or a person can mean or intend to be negligent by falsely damaging another's reputation.

In all cases, we are concerned basically with disregarding the
safety of others. We all have a right to expect others to treat us
with reasonable caution. Of course we must also look out for
our own safety. When we contribute to our own injury, even
though another person was also careless, we may lose our rights
to sue and recover damages.   In the case of "contributory
negligence," age is also a factor.

Suppose a seventeen-year-old runs into the street chasing a
Frisbee and a speeding car hits her, breaking her leg. Probably
that young woman cannot successfully sue the speeder; her
failure to look out for her own safety was a contributing factor
in her injury. If, however, she was six or seven instead of seven-
teen, then the law will likely say that, as a young child, she was
incapable of contributory negligence, and the negligent speeder
may be held liable. The operator of an automobile is obligated
to look out for small children as they generally do not look out
for themselves. Makes sense, doesn't it?

When a minor is engaged in activity that is considered "adult" in nature, he may be held to adult standards of conduct regardless of age. Thus, a sixteen-year-old driving an automobile will generally not benefit from a presumption that, due to his youth, he was non-negligent.

There are some civil wrongs, torts, that may occur in connection with a contract. In these cases, a minor may not be held liable for damages because of the legal doctrine that he cannot enter into contracts. Suppose a minor rents a floor waxer and, through carelessness, the machine is damaged beyond repair. The renting agency hasn't sound grounds for a suit against the girl for her negligence because the basis of the arrangement was a rental contract. It should be added that some courts have decided against minors in such cases when they have misrepresented their ages when the contracts were made.

As a general rule, the damages that may be recovered in a negligence lawsuit include medical bills, earnings lost while the injured person is recovering and, if the injuries are permanent, money the plaintiff would have earned in the future if he or she had not been hurt. In some cases, a jury might also award damages to compensate for the pain caused by the injury.

In the case of "intentional" torts, such as libel or slander (written or spoken words that damage a person's reputation), a defendant may have to pay punitive damages. This category of damages refers to money over and above what the plaintiff actually lost as a result of the injury. They are intended to punish the defendant to prevent his doing the same thing again. As a rule, a minor will not be assessed punitive damages, the courts feeling that, due to youth and inexperience, the minor cannot appreciate the harm that he or she intentionally inflicted. In such cases, the courts may also reason that, since the parents usually have to pay, the child will not "feel" the punishment in any event.

What role do parents play in the legal field of tort law? Depending on state law, a child may or may not be able to sue in his or her own name. In practice and by rule in the federal courts, it is the court's responsibility to be certain that a minor is properly represented. This will usually mean that a minor must sue in the name of a parent or a guardian.

How does a person start a lawsuit? To sue another person or a company who we believe has injured us, we must, in most cases, "file" a document with the clerk of the court stating briefly what wrong was done, how we were damaged and how much money we think we deserve to be paid because of the injury. In almost all cases, the suit papers are prepared by a lawyer and a filing fee will have to be paid to the clerk.

Our suit papers then must be served or given to the person we claim caused the injury. The person filing the suit, again, is the plaintiff and the person or party who is sued is the defendant. The defendant will then have to file an answer to our suit. Usually the defendant's answer will deny the claims of the plaintiff. Additional documents may be filed by both sides, seeking information about each other's case. These must be answered within certain time limits. All of the papers filed in a lawsuit are known as the "pleadings."

When the opponents have prepared their case, a trial will be scheduled. They, their lawyers and their witnesses will, on the date the trial is "set," go to the courtroom and present their claims to the jury or, if both sides agree, to the judge without a jury.

What is a jury? It is a group of men and women chosen at random from the community. They are responsible for deciding the facts of the case. Always the opposing sides have different versions of what the facts were. A defendant in an automobile accident case may say that he put on his brakes and he may call a witness who will testify, under oath, that she saw his brake lights go on. The plaintiff will try to disprove this evidence by presenting evidence that, for instance, the defendant's car left no skid marks. The jury must consider the evidence from both sides and decide what actually happened.

The defendant in a criminal case is guaranteed a jury by both the Constitution and the Bill of Rights. In civil cases, the right to a jury is preserved by Article 7 of the Bill of Rights in all cases involving twenty dollars or more. The right to a jury is one of our basic freedoms. If we value this freedom, as we should, we must also honor our duty to serve on a jury when called. Almost everyone, at some time in his or her life, will be asked to be a juror. Although it may be a hardship, we must agree to give our time if we value our basic rights and wish to preserve them.

The judge, when the parties have chosen a jury, must decide the law applicable to the case. He determines what evidence is trustworthy and can be presented to the jury. If, in our accident case, the witness says that she wasn't at the scene of the accident but that other persons told her they saw the brake lights go on, the judge may not "admit" such testimony because it is "hearsay." He will not let the jury consider second hand information.

At the end of the trial, the judge will tell or "instruct" the members of the jury what the law is and how they should apply it to the facts of the case in reaching their decision or "verdict." Thus he may tell the jury that "if you find from the facts that the plaintiff entered the intersection without looking and observing oncoming traffic, then the plaintiff was contributorily negligent and he may not recover against the defendant."

After being instructed as to the law, the jury "retires" to its jury room to consider the facts and the judge's instructions and decide the case. The jury's task is not easy for, in most cases that go to a trial, there is strong evidence on both sides. While the system is sometimes difficult and not always perfect, it has proven over the centuries to be reliable and worthy of our trust. But now, What about you? How is a minor treated in a lawsuit?

In civil cases the courts invariably require an adult to serve as guardian to a minor involved in a lawsuit. Usually the guardian is the child's parent. It is the guardian's responsibility to properly control the course of the litigation; that is to consult with the minor's lawyer and make decisions regarding the handling of the case. A failure on his part to properly perform this duty can result in his removal and replacement by the court. It is the court's responsibility, and not the minor's, to determine whether the lawyer representing the child is doing his or her job correctly.

In the case of a minor plaintiff, his parents may recover damages for his injuries in addition to what he may receive. Parents may recover the cost of a child's medical treatment and care. A minor's lost earnings are recoverable not by the child but by his parents since they, by law, are entitled to his "services" until he becomes an adult.

The child may recover, in his own name, damages awarded as a result of pain or suffering. If the minor sustains any permanent injury which will reduce his earning capacity once he reaches adulthood, he may recover a projected amount based upon what he will reasonably be expected to lose during his adult working life.

An award of damages assumes that that the child and those guiding and representing him have successfully proved their case. A defendant, of course, may win the case by proving to the jury's satisfaction that it was not negligent at all. As in our example above, the defendant may raise a defense such as contributory negligence that would prevent a recovery. Such a defense would apply not only to the suit by the child represented by the guardian but also to the parent's action for loss of services and medical care.

Settlement

Often a person who is involved in a legal dispute will agree to a compromise before a lawsuit is filed or, even if it is filed, before it goes to a trial. This is true of legal problems arising not only in the field of torts but in almost every other field of the law. Seldom does a case arise in which one party is absolutely right and the other is absolutely wrong. Lawyers are under an obligation to closely analyze all the facts of each client's case and then consider those facts in the light of the law. A lawyer is free of the emotional pressure that a client often feels and, therefore, can evaluate the problem objectively.

Once a case has been studied by the attorney, he or she will be aware of its good and bad points and should have a reasonably good idea of what the result will be if the problem is finally resolved in court. Based on their conclusions, the attorneys for the persons involved in the dispute will meet and see if they can work out a compromise.

A compromise of a legal dispute, frequently called a settlement, should always be in the best interest of the client the lawyer represents. The Canons of the American Bar Association, *Code of Professional Responsibility* (1969), which govern a lawyer's conduct, advise that "The professional judgment of a lawyer should be exercised, within the bounds of law, solely for the benefit of his client and free of compromising influences and loyalties." A lawyer must not compromise a case because of his own self interest, because he does not have time to go to trial, because he will not earn a sufficient fee, or because he does not want to embarrass or harm his opponent. Only the strengths and weaknesses of his client's case, weighed independently of all other considerations, should affect his efforts to compromise.

On the other hand, settlement is a proper goal if it is in the client's best interest. Abraham Lincoln, a lawyer, said "Discourage litigation. Persuade your neighbors to compromise whenever you can. Point out to them how the nominal winner is often a real loser—in fees, expenses and waste of time. As a peacemaker, the lawyer has a superior opportunity of being a good man. Never stir up litigation. A worse man can scarcely be found than one who does this."

In compromising a case before or after the filing of a lawsuit, the injured person will be paid a mutually agreed upon sum of money by the person he claims is responsible for his damages. A "release" is given in exchange for the payment. This document, signed by the person claiming he was injured, acknowledges receipt of the money. It also states that he gives up all claims he has against the other person. That is, he gives up the claims based upon the circumstances which caused his injury.

A release is not an admission of fault on the part of the person paying the money nor is it an admission on the part of the person receiving the money that he was not damaged as badly as he originally claimed. A release is only a contract reflecting a compromise whereby, in consideration for a sum of money, the plaintiff gives up all claims against the defendant.

When a case involving a minor is compromised, particularly when a lawsuit has been filed, the court may be requested to approve the settlement. A person charged with damaging another certainly does not want to settle a case unless he is absolutely certain that the release is final and binding. For this reason, a minor does not usually sign a release or, if he does, it is also signed by his parent or legal guardian. To be absolutely certain that the settlement is final and not subject to challenge after the minor reaches adulthood, a court's approval is almost always necessary.

If a lawsuit has not been filed, an action will have to be filed to obtain the court's approval. Although the opponents have settled their differences, they must also satisfy the court that the settlement is fair to the minor and that the money paid for the minor's injury will be protected and used for his benefit.

The judge's primary obligation is to protect the interest of the minor. To accomplish this, a hearing may be held to review the facts of the case. Once the court analyzes the case and determines that the settlement is fair and reasonable, it will enter a final order approving the compromise and dismissing the case "with prejudice." These last two words mean that another suit on the same claim may never be filed again. These procedures are applicable whether the minor is the party claiming damages or is the person against whom the claim is made.

Chapter 10

THE JUVENILE COURTS

We have described the activities and purposes of civil courts. We now turn to the juvenile courts. They deal with activity which, if carried out by an adult, would be considered criminal.

Many people think that the improvement of our system of juvenile criminal justice is the greatest challenge and most important task in the law today. This is based on the belief that a great portion of adult crime has its roots in juvenile delinquency. The time to avoid dangerous behavior in later life is at the juvenile level. This may involve improved handling of young offenders or, better yet, providing children the kind of guidance needed to prevent their becoming offenders. In most cases, a juvenile court proceeding provides a young person with his first look at the country's legal system; a new world of courtrooms, lawyers and judges.

While few would disagree that there is need for improvement, there are many, many different views as to how this goal can be reached.

It is a purpose of this book to describe our system of law as it exists today. There are many changes in progress in the field of criminal justice and, particularly, as it concerns the young. Systems once thought progressive are under attack today, but to review proposed reforms or suggest alternatives is not within the scope of this book.

The Honorable William E. MacFaden, a juvenile judge in Los

Angeles, wrote in *Crime and Delinquency*, published by the National Council on Crime and Delinquency (April, 1971), that:

> Perhaps our greatest fault in dealing with minors is our assumption, when the minor nods his head or agrees with our statements, that he understands, when in fact he may have no comprehension of our gibberish but believes that we want him to agree with us and that to do so will help him.

It is our purpose here to assist the minor in understanding the juvenile court system. Whether a person is in the hands of the system, seeks to improve it or only to criticize it, an understanding of what it consists of now is the vital first step.

Traditionally, a minor charged with a crime was treated in the same way as an adult. Assuming that a child was old enough to know right from wrong, he was arrested, prosecuted and, if convicted, he was punished in the same manner as an adult. Early codes specified age 7 as the "age of criminal responsibility."

Our present system represents a departure from those laws which treated children as adults where crime was concerned. The various systems of juvenile justice found in our country today were enacted as reforms by our state and Federal legislatures in the early 1900's. These reforms are under constant review and different states, as well as the Federal courts, approach the problem of juvenile crime in different ways. Frequently we hear of new programs developed by different localities and described variously as the "Illinois plan" or the "California system" or by other titles. All of these represent attempts to find solutions to the problem. The easy lesson is that what might be true in New York may very well be different in Colorado. Further, each state system is subject to change every time the legislature meets so, whether you've moved from one state to another or not, what was the law yesterday may not be the law today.

An adult charged with a crime is guaranteed certain basic rights by the United States Constitution. The accused is protected by the first ten amendments to the United States Constitution, known as the "Bill of Rights." These rules of procedure state how a person is to be tried for a crime. Among other protections, they specify that a person suspected of a crime is entitled to a speedy trial, to be confronted by his accusers, to have a lawyer and to have his guilt or innocence determined by a jury.

Due Process

The Fifth and Fourteenth Amendments state that no person shall, by either the Federal or State governments, be deprived of his life, liberty or property without "due process of law." This phrase has been interpreted broadly by the courts in rejecting criminal laws that are too confusing to be understood. They have also required notice and hearings as to any government action which could result in the loss of one's liberty or his property or property rights. Due process demands that all laws apply in the same way to all people. No single definition can fully describe due process. It is a comprehensive phrase said to be rooted in common law traditions of fairness and honesty.

The manner in which our legal differences are resolved is known as the adversary system. As we have said, the trial is the point at which the two opposing sides come face to face with each other. The judge is the impartial "referee" responsible for applying the law to the contest before him. The jury determines the facts and decides which side wins. This is true in criminal law as well as civil law. In criminal cases, the state and the accused are literally against each other; they are adversaries. This is not true of our juvenile court systems.

Reform

When the states enacted their reform laws creating juvenile

courts, it was felt that minors should not be subject to an adversary form of justice. The legislation, in effect, established an entirely new system designed to eliminate the idea that the state, in its role as the protector of children should be "for" the child, and the juvenile judge is the protector of the minor charged with criminal conduct.

Although the juvenile criminal justice systems, through their juvenile courts, can and do punish, that is not said to be their primary goal. Their purpose is to protect, correct and reform. In this way, they are specialized courts, apart from our traditional civil and criminal courts but combining elements of each. A purpose in establishing juvenile justice systems is to separate minors from adults at all stages from arrest through trial, custody and the process of correction.

In trying to accomplish these goals, a special legal terminology has developed. Different from one state to another, a minor who has violated a law is not a "criminal" or a "defendant" but a juvenile delinquent or offender. A juvenile court does not find a minor "guilty" but rather "not innocent" or "within the purview of the court." Proceedings in juvenile court are said to be civil rather than criminal. In a majority of cases, hearings are private and informal and no publicity is permitted and no public record made of the juvenile court's actions.

We would ignore both reality and recent decisions of the United States Supreme Court if we did not say that this system has been criticized and is undergoing court-directed change at this time.

You will recall our description earlier of the constitutional rights to which everyone accused of a crime is entitled. Until the recent past, it was felt that these rights did not apply to minors in juvenile courts. Since a juvenile court was considered a civil rather than a criminal court, removed from the adversary system, the juvenile proceedings were looked upon as being subject only to the requirement of due process. The general reasoning was that, since the court was the protector of the child, he did not need and was not entitled to a lawyer or the other safeguards provided by the Bill of Rights. In the informal treatment of cases before them, the courts were given wide leeway in seeing that a minor was treated fairly.

Recent Changes

There is no doubt that the legislation creating juvenile justice systems arose from an honest concern for the young person in trouble with the law. Nevertheless, the freedom granted juvenile courts to deal informally and in private with juvenile offenders has not proven satisfactory.

It has been recognized that a minor and his or her parents must have notice of what the charges against the child are. They need a lawyer to advise them as to the meaning of the charges and what they should do. Children subject to commitment to a state institution, be it a vocational school, forestry camp or state farm, are entitled to the same protections given an adult accused of a crime.

This was the ruling of the United States Supreme Court in a case known as *In re Gault* decided in 1967. That decision marked a change in the law of juvenile justice that is still in the process of development. The decision is long and complex but, nevertheless, essential reading for any student of the law of minors.

The *Gault* case leaves undisturbed the principle that the juvenile system must remain separate from the adult system. It also recognizes the need for privacy and a degree of informality in juvenile cases. But, the court recognizes that these good points can be kept while still granting the basic protection found in the Bill of Rights.

At one point in its decision, the court said, "Under our Constitution, the condition of being a boy does not justify a kangaroo court." These are words that stir emotions and hopefully will cast some doubt on the general belief that the law is dry and dusty if not altogether dead. The decision should not be read as a slap in the face of our juvenile courts where thousands of dedicated judges, clerks, probation and youth correction officers labor long hours in overcrowded courtrooms. It is the role of our courts, including our highest court, to guide us, to protect us, and to safeguard our constitutional guarantees. The laws which create our judicial systems and, thus, the legislatures that enact the laws must always be subject to that final guidance.

The Juvenile Courts Today

Let us look now at the juvenile court itself. These are not civil courts but are courts that deal primarily with wrongs against the state and community. We may soon realize why these courts are so busy. Juvenile courts have jurisdiction over both felony cases and misdemeanors in which minors are involved. This jurisdiction includes violations of criminal laws that apply to young and old alike, ranging from murder and burglary in the felony class down to disorderly conduct and traffic violations which are misdemeanors.

These courts also deal with violations of laws that apply only to minors, such as curfew violations, falsifying the age shown on identification cards, and truancy. These violations that are violations only because of the offender's juvenile status are called "status offenses." The juvenile courts also deal with adults who involve minors in criminal conduct. Such conduct is a violation of the criminal codes often known as "contributing to the delinquency of a minor."

Adults who harm children either intentionally, through abuse, or unintentionally, by neglect or abandonment, come under a juvenile court's jurisdiction. These courts are also concerned with problems arising as the result of divorces, particularly in cases involving a former husband and father who fails to support his family.

All of the foregoing relate to violations of a law in one form or another.   Beyond this, juvenile courts frequently handle matters such as the commitment of minors suffering from mental illness and emergency surgical or medical treatment for minors whose parents are unavailable.

In some states, a separate juvenile court with its own court-rooms and judges may be established. In others, those courts having jurisdiction over minors and their problems may be "divisions" of a general court system. A number of states separate juvenile cases from those which concern purely the family and marital problems, calling the latter "Domestic Relations" courts.

The Juvenile Case

A case is usually brought before the juvenile court by a petition naming the minor and stating the nature of the offense he is charged with or the problem that the court is being asked to resolve. In the typical situation, the petition may be filed by a parent, an officer of the court such as a probation officer or any other "interested party." Normally the petition must be "verified," that is, signed under oath.

Once the petition is received by the court, a summons may be issued to the minor, his parents or other persons involved. Even though the parents are not directly involved, as in the case of misbehavior in school, they, nevertheless, are summoned to court. In the event the petition indicates an emergency situation presenting danger to the minor or to others, the court may order that he be taken into immediate custody and held until the case comes before the court.

Juvenile cases involving a wrong that may result in serious punishment for the offender are usually held in two stages. The first stage involves a hearing to determine whether the minor involved is within the court's jurisdiction, whether a lawyer is desired, and whether in fact the offense was committed. If the minor or his parents cannot afford a lawyer, the court will appoint one to represent him.

Correction

The second stage of the proceeding concerns the disposition of the case. If the court has determined that the law was broken, it must next decide what must be done to correct the wrong. As we have said earlier, the person charged with an offense in juvenile court may not be the minor himself; it may be that an adult has committed the wrong. The solution, however, will generally involve the young person concerned. Thus, if the court finds that a parent has abandoned or neglected a child, it may take the child into custody, place him or her in a foster home or take such other steps as will protect the child's welfare.

If the child is the offender, the court may take the child into custody and place him in a state institution; it may order a fine or put him under probation. If someone's property was damaged, as in the case of vandalism, the court might well order the juvenile offender to pay for the damage. This remedy is known as "restitution."

Juvenile courts traditionally have a great deal of freedom in the area of correction, and the foregoing is by no means the only action that they can take. A court may assign juvenile offenders to weekend work with a city's park maintenance department or it might direct that they report each Friday to work for the person whose property they have damaged.

Background Investigation

In any case, an extremely important part of the procedure takes place in between the first courtroom hearing and the second. In most states, once the court has reached its first decision, an investigation is conducted by the court's staff into the background of the minor. This investigation concerns the physical well-being of the child, his school record, his home life and the circumstances of the offense for which he has been found responsible.

The results of the investigation are gathered together in a report and submitted to the court for the judge's consideration before he reaches his decision.

Probation

Probation is a remedy the courts frequently use in juvenile courts. The word comes from the Latin word *probatio* meaning proof. The probation system establishes a set period of time during which a minor must prove that he or she can behave properly.

A court may place a minor on supervised or unsupervised probation. In the case of unsupervised probation, the minor remains under the control of his or her parents only. In the event the probationer misbehaves, fails to attend school regularly, or does not come home, the parents should report these facts to the court. Probation can then be revoked and the minor taken into custody for such action as the court may feel is required.

Supervised probation is a form of combined custody. The parents in such situations are responsible for day-to-day conduct but, periodically, the minor must report to a probation officer. In this way, the court keeps a close watch over the youth's activities. A failure to report can result in the revocation of the probation.

Probation officers are trained specialists in dealing with the young. They are responsible to the court and report regularly as to the progress of the minors they are responsible for.

What we have described here is the "typical" handling of a case. As we have said earlier, there are different systems of juvenile justice. There are also many undecided questions which may finally have to be answered by the courts. For example, a minor subject to the jurisdiction of a juvenile court is not presently entitled to a jury trial should he desire one. This is just one of the questions that have not yet been decided.

Adult Treatment

Another important function of a juvenile court is its power to determine, in the case of a serious offense, that a minor may be treated as an adult and, therefore, is subject to the same procedure as an adult accused of a crime. Statues granting this power vary from state to state. In some areas, the juvenile courts have no jurisdiction over "capital offenses," that is, those crimes that may be punished by life imprisonment or death. In other states, the juvenile courts are granted the power to decide whether to keep the case in the juvenile court or to send the accused on to the general criminal courts for prosecution and, if found guilty, punished as an adult.

Where the juvenile courts have the freedom to keep the case or send it on, the decision is generally based upon whether the judge believes that the rehabilitation provided at the juvenile level is going to be of greater benefit than the punishment generally found in the "adult" system.

In determining these and related questions, a hearing is required. The minor and his parents are entitled to notice of the hearing; they have the right to be present, the right to a lawyer and the right to examine the state's evidence.

If a minor's case is sent to the court having general criminal jurisdiction, he or she will, as we have stated, be subject to prosecution and, if guilty, punishment in the same manner and to the same degree as an adult. The fact that the accused is a minor may have some bearing on the proof necessary to show intent to commit a crime. Nevertheless, a minor being tried as an adult may raise, as a defense, his age, and the prosecution must show that he is capable, in spite of age, of understanding the nature of the crime he is charged with.

Chapter 11

CRIMINAL LAW

Criminal justice is as old as mankind itself. The Bible and earlier writings offer repeated descriptions of the manner in which those who harmed others were tried and sentenced by kings, priests and conquerors. Our present system is founded on the early common law; but, as developed today, it is largely set forth in statutes enacted by our legislatures.

Federal and State Jurisdiction of Criminal Law

Federal laws as well as state laws specify those actions which are criminal and which society, through the courts, will punish. Federal crimes often concern illegal activities that are interstate in nature. Kidnapping, hijacking and bank robbery are examples of Federal crimes that frequently involve activity in more than one state.

Federal laws and law enforcement officers also concern themselves with crimes involving the theft of government property, the forgery of government documents and counterfeiting of United States currency. Crimes that violate Federal laws such as income tax evasion and fraud, gambling and the manufacture of untaxed alcoholic beverages are the concern of Federal criminal law. All of these crimes are handled by our Federal court system and may be punished by imprisonment in Federal penitentiaries.

Depending entirely on the legislation defining the crime, certain offenses may fall solely within the power of the Federal system, solely within the State system or be subject to both. State laws often cover the same areas as Federal laws and Federal laws provide that persons on government property are subject to the criminal laws of the State in which the base or installation is located. Where both systems have jurisdiction their powers are said to be "concurrent." In such cases, the authorities first involved in detection and arrest will maintain control over the prosecution of the accused and their punishment if found guilty. In some situations, conduct which originally appears to be subject to only State law may become a Federal matter, as where those suspected of a crime cross State lines in carrying out their crime or avoiding arrest.

Constitutional Rights

The person accused of a crime is known as the defendant just as the person sued in a civil case is also a defendant. It is important to understand that a defendant accused of a crime for the first time is *not* a criminal and should not be referred to as a criminal. It is basic to our common law tradition and our constitutional foundation that a person is innocent until proven guilty. Why is this?

The very heart of our democratic system is our liberty, our freedom to peacefully lead our individual lives. Only when we breach the peace, break the law, can we be deprived of that liberty. Since liberty is of vital importance to us as citizens of a democracy, it is of supreme importance that the process by which one's freedom is taken must be absolutely fair. The State has the duty to preserve the peace for all of us and therefore it has the obligation to punish those who break our laws. It is important to each of us that the State fulfill its responsibilities in keeping with our Constitution.

Due Process

If one person can be sent to jail without a fair trail, denied a lawyer, compelled to testify against himself, denied the right to confront witnesses against him or be found guilty without a jury, then each of us can be treated in the same manner. Those rights found in the Constitution's Bill of Rights, are intended to protect the innocent. They are intended to safeguard our liberty. They insure that, before one can be denied his freedom, that State must fully and fairly prove his or her guilt.

The extent to which these rights will be applied in a particular case is the subject of constant study by our courts. Let us look at several examples.

A sixteen-year-old witness for the State saw two men standing near the place where a stolen safe was found. One of the men, the boy testified, had a crowbar in his hand. The boy had identified a defendant as being one of the men he had seen. The defense attorney, faced with this damaging evidence, sought to discredit the young man's testimony by introducing evidence that he was a juvenile offender who was on probation for two burglaries at the time he testified. The trial court refused to allow such evidence on the basis that a juvenile's record was confidential under state law. The United States Supreme Court reversed the case. They held that the Sixth Amendment right of an accused to confront his witness includes the right to fully question the witness by cross-examination. "In this setting," the Court stated, "we conclude that the right of confrontation is paramount to the State's policy of protecting a juvenile offender."

In another case, a police officer stopped a young man for driving at night without lights. The car was searched, but nothing objectionable was found. The driver was not arrested for the traffic offense but received a summons to traffic court. Apparently the officer had some doubts as to the ownership of the car, so he took the boy into custody and turned him over to the juvenile authorities. Five hours later he was searched and a small amount of loose "green substance" was found in his pocket.

At his hearing, over the objections of the boy's lawyer, a police laboratory representative testified that the substance was marijuana and the court found him delinquent.

The Court of Civil Appeals of Texas reversed the decision on the grounds that the search, five hours after the original traffic offense occurred and having nothing to do with the traffic ticket, was in violation of the Fourth Amendment prohibition against illegal search and seizure. Evidence obtained by illegal search is not admissable in court and the juvenile court was mistaken in denying the lawyer's objections.

The general rule is that a police officer, having stopped a person for a traffic offense, can search the car and make an arrest for another offense if he or she discovers evidence in open view or has probable cause to believe that a more serious crime has been committed. Otherwise the police officer must first acquire a warrant for arrest and, if a search is desired, obtain a search warrant.

The Texas court, in reference to the Fourth Amendment protection against search and seizure, said, "A minor has the same constitutional right to be secure in his person from all unreasonable seizures as has an adult."

Resisting arrest

Our laws protect a person against false arrest. Even if an arrest is not justified, the person being arrested should refrain from using force to resist arrest. Such resistance makes the accused the judge of whether his or her arrest is lawful. This could lead to violence and chaos. Even "passive resistance" or "going limp" has been held to be resistance to arrest and is a punishable offense as obstruction of justice.

Waiver

When a person voluntarily gives up his rights, he is said to have "waived" his rights. A person accused of a crime may waive any of his constitutional rights either by expressly saying that he chooses to do so or by doing or saying something that clearly shows he is doing so.

Upon arrest, an accused person is invariably informed by the arresting officer that he has the right to a lawyer and the right to remain silent. If then the accused discusses his involvement in the crime, he has waived the right to self-incrimination. An accused person may consent to a search of his person or his apartment. If, through the search following consent, the police discover evidence of a crime, that evidence is admissible at trial.

At the trial itself, a defendant may waive his right to a jury and, in such cases, the court has the duty of deciding the facts and the law, determining guilt or innocence and, if guilt is found, passing sentence.

The act of waiving, known as waiver with regard to one's constitutional rights, is a serious step, and the courts are very careful to be certain that the accused fully understands what he is doing; that he is not under the influence of drugs and acts voluntarily without force or without promise.

Arrest

From the foregoing, we gain some information about arrests, and it is a good point to turn our discussion to a more detailed consideration of the criminal process itself.

Crimes are carefully defined by our criminal codes and, in order to find a defendant guilty, each element of the crime must be proved to the jury. At the time a crime is suspected, however, the police must quickly analyze the facts available, question witnesses and determine from this evidence who the person is who probably committed it. The process may take minutes when a jewelry store window is smashed and eye witnesses can identify the person who did it. It may take months when the crime is illegal gambling or the sale of heroin and undercover police work is necessary.

When the police witness the commission of a crime, have a reasonable belief that a person they suspect of criminal conduct is going to escape or perhaps injure others, they may make an immediate arrest. Where these dangers do not exist, a warrant must be obtained which specifically identifies the crime charged and the facts upon which the charge is based. A warrant is issued by a court only after a formal complaint or charge has been filed. Generally the person filing a criminal charge must provide a sworn written statement—an affidavit which forms the basis for the warrant. The warrant itself directs a police officer to take the accused into custody, and he has no alternative but to do so once it is in his hands.

In the case of some misdemeanors and traffic offenses, a formal arrest is not made. The accused receives a summons or citation and signs a statement promising to appear in court on a certain date. In such cases, the signing is not an admission of guilt. If the charged party refuses to sign the document, the officer has no alternative but to take the person into custody.

Preliminary Hearing

Once an accused is arrested and taken into custody, he is without unreasonable delay taken before a judge or court official and formally charged with the crime described in the warrant. The judge or, in federal courts, the magistrate conducts a preliminary examination of the accused. This generally includes a determination of the identity of the accused, further advice as to constitutional rights, and the appointment of a lawyer if the defendant cannot afford one. In most states the examination is a full hearing at which the person who obtained the warrant or the arresting officer, if no warrant was required, testifies as to the basic facts upon which the charge is based. The accused in such cases is entitled to a lawyer and may cross-examine the witnesses against him. If he does not have a lawyer, the court may postpone or "continue" the case to another day, enabling the defendant to retain one. If he cannot, the court will appoint counsel to represent him.

The primary purpose of such hearings is to determine whether there is "probable cause" to believe a crime has been committed and that the defendant was involved in its commission.

This step in the procedure is not a determination of guilt or innocence any more than an arrest is a determination of guilt or innocence. The court may not find an accused guilty. It may dismiss the case altogether if, for instance, the person who obtained the warrant did not appear or there was insufficient evidence that the person arrested committed the crime. In many jurisdictions, the judge conducting the examination has the power to change the charge from a felony to a misdemeanor if the facts justify such a step. The examining judge in such cases, may, having jurisdiction over misdemeanor charges, then proceed to try the defendant on the reduced charge.

If, on the other hand, the court finds that probable cause exists that a crime was committed and that the accused committed it, he will determine next whether bail will be permitted and in what amount.

Bail

Bail refers usually to an amount of money which the accused gives or "posts" as security for his appearance at his trial. Once bail is posted with the clerk of the court, the accused may be released from custody. In many cases, a bail bond in the amount set by the court is purchased by the accused from a professional bail bondsman. This is in effect a specialized form of an insurance policy. The bondsman agrees, in return for a premium paid by the defendant to the bondsman, that he will pay the court the full amount of the bail if the defendant doesn't come to court when he is supposed to.

If the crime the defendant is charged with is not a serious one, if the defendant has a job and family, has a good record and appears reliable, the amount of the bond may be fairly low. If some or all of these factors are not present, the amount of the bail may be higher. The bail bondsman may not wish to take a risk and can refuse to post bond in which case the defendant or his family and friends will have to raise the actual amount of money and post it with the clerk as security for release.

A court may release a defendant on his own personal "recognizance" without requiring bail as security. This means that he is simply on his personal honor to return to court when the court directs him and no bail is required. Many states are now experimenting with new programs which substantially reduce or eliminate bail altogether. These efforts based upon the theory that, guilty or innocent, defendants seldom will risk flight to escape trial and placing them under a heavy financial burden only serves to put the family in debt.

Grand Jury

Following the preliminary examination, many jurisdictions provide that the case must go before a "grand jury." This is a court-appointed group of citizens who have the responsibility of inquiring into the facts surrounding crimes committed in their locality and determining the probable guilt or innocence of the accused.

At first this appears to be a duplication of the function performed at the preliminary examination. History tells us, however, that the grand jury is a check by the citizens on the power of the state.

The court is an arm of the state government, and the grand jury continues today to assure that one's fellow citizens, in addition to the state, have the opportunity to review criminal charges and thereby determine whether they are properly brought. If the grand jury finds probable cause that the accused committed the crime he or she is charged with, an "indictment" or "true bill" is issued. This is a formal accusation intended to fully describe the crime so that the defendant may prepare a proper defense.

There are instances in which grand juries issue indictments before arrest. Such cases usually involve complex criminal operations requiring the police to move quickly and with an element of surprise in order to arrest all suspected participants. In such cases, the preliminary examination is still held but is more limited in scope, generally dealing only with the appointment of counsel and setting bail.

Special grand juries may be appointed by the court for particular purposes. In these instances, they investigate and, if they decide that crimes are being committed, they return indictments or "presentments." These formal charges recommend specific governmental actions to prevent criminal activity. Such grand juries may be appointed to investigate corruption in government or scandals involving public officials.

Where state law does not provide for a grand jury system, the state or locality's legal department, prosecuting attorney, or district attorney may obtain an "information" to be filed with the court. This, like the grand jury's indictment, formally accuses the defendant and informs him as well as the court of the facts upon which the charge is based. In grand jury states a defendant may waive grand jury, and the case will then proceed on the prosecuting attorney's information.

Chapter 12

CRIMINAL LAW – THE TRIAL AND PUNISHMENT

We have noted that an arrest is the act of taking a person into custody in a legal manner. As also noted, if investigation shows there is enough of a case to go further, the person is formally charged so that he may prepare to defend himself.

Trial

Once properly charged, a defendant is brought to trial. The proceeding generally opens with the "arraignment" of the accused. This is the point at which the full charge is read and the defendant is asked how he "pleads." His response may be either guilty or not guilty. With the court's permission, a defendant may be permitted to plead "nolo contendere." By such a plea, the accused avoids a direct admission of guilt or a claim of innocence but says that he simply will not challenge the facts against him; he will leave the decision up to the court. This plea is most frequently used to avoid an admission that might be used against the accused in another case, either civil or criminal.

If the plea is guilty, the court will proceed to hear the case, without a jury, to determine for itself whether the plea is proper, and what punishment should be imposed. If the plea is not guilty the trial will proceed with the selection of a jury or, if the defendant has waived his right to a jury, opening statements by the defense and prosecution and thereafter the presentation of evidence.

If the defendant wants a jury, he may participate through his attorney in the selection of those who will serve on the jury that will decide the case. This jury is completely different from a grand jury and is not involved at all in pre-trial activity. It is selected from a larger number of citizens known as a jury panel. The panel is selected in various ways depending on state law. In some instances, a jury commission is appointed by the local city council or county board which has the duty of accumulating lists of persons qualified to serve. The names may be taken at random from the tax rolls, voter registration lists or other similar sources.

A criminal jury consists of twelve persons. For each trial, a larger number are called to court. The judge, the defense lawyer, and the prosecuting attorney can each ask questions of the potential jurors to determine whether they have any bias toward either the state or the accused. If there is a reason why they would be unable to reach an impartial verdict, they will be excused from the jury.

With the jury chosen, the trial proceeds. Trial procedure is complex and cannot be described in detail here. Several important points may be mentioned. The defendant must be present at all times both at trial and at any hearings that may be held before trial.

Frequently trials turn on whether certain evidence will be allowed, and the court may wish to decide these questions before the trial begins, to avoid lengthy arguments during which the jury must "retire" to the jury room. Accordingly, court rules often require that certain defenses be brought up and decided before the actual trial begins.

The defendant may, by pre-trial motion, claim that he was forced to sign a confession or that evidence against him was obtained by an illegal search or seizure. In such a case, he may make a motion to "suppress" the confession or the evidence. If the court agrees with the accused, the prosecution will be unable to present the confession or the evidence during the trial.

A "motion" is a request made to the judge asking him to do a particular thing. At the opening of a trial, for example, a lawyer may "move" the court to require all witnesses to leave the courtroom so that they will not hear what the other witnesses say on the witness stand. If the judge "grants" the motion, he will order all witnesses to go out of the courtroom to await their call to testify.

The prosecution presents its evidence first and the defense is entitled to question, through cross-examination, each of the prosecution's witnesses. It is the prosecution's task to prove the defendant's guilt "beyond a reasonable doubt." This is a higher degree of proof than is necessary to establish liability in a civil case.

Once the prosecution completes its case or "rests," it is usual for the defense lawyer to make a motion to the effect that the court should acquit the defendant because, based on the law, the prosecution has failed to prove its case. The state must prove every element of the crime as stated in the indictment or information. If it plainly fails to do this, the court may rule that, under such circumstances, the jury could not find the defendant guilty and dismiss the case without its going to the jury for decision.

This point brings up the question of double jeopardy. The United States Constitution and most state constitutions provide that a person once tried for an offense may not be placed in jeopardy a second time for the same offense. "Jeopardy" generally means "danger." In other words, a person who has faced the peril of conviction cannot be placed in danger of being again convicted for the same crime.

A defendant is not considered in jeopardy unless his trial has actually started. Nor is a defendant able to plead prior jeopardy when the first court that tried him did not have proper jurisdiction. Thus, if a defendant was brought to trial, pleaded guilty and was sentenced in a court that had no power over him, he could be tried over again in the proper court. A defendant must plead double jeopardy before his second trial or he will be ruled to have waived his rights.

Once the prosecution finishes or "rests," the defense presents its evidence in support of the defendant's innocence. The prosecuting attorney can cross-examine the defense witnesses and, once the defense rests, present additional evidence on new issues raised by the defense.

When both sides are finished, the court, if there is a jury, must "instruct" the jury as to what law applies to the case and how the jury should decide the facts in keeping with the law. If, for instance, the defendant has introduced evidence that he was not at the scene of the crime, a portion of the court's instruction might be:

> Evidence has been introduced tending to establish an alibi, which amounts to a contention that the defendant was not present at the time when or at the place where he is alleged to have committed the offense charged in the indictment.

> If, after consideration of all the evidence in the case, you have a reasonable doubt as to whether the defendant was present at the time and place the alleged offense was committed, you must acquit him.

The judge decides what his instructions will be after meeting with the prosecution and defense lawyers. They request certain instructions and the judge may or may not grant their requests.

In final arguments to the jury, the lawyer for the prosecution and the lawyer for the defense summarize the evidence, point out the weak points in the opponent's case and try to persuade the jury to agree. Once the instructions are given and arguments finished, the jury "retires" to decide the guilt or innocence of the defendant. Of course, when there is no jury, the judge hears the arguments and decides the case.

The jury in a federal criminal trial does not decide how the defendant shall be punished if its verdict is guilty. The "sentence" or punishment is decided by the judge, usually after a pre-sentence investigation and report have been completed by the federal probation service. The investigation report provides information regarding the defendant's prior criminal record, his health, employment and family. A report is obtained whether or not the case was tried with a jury.

In many state systems, the jury not only determines guilt or innocence but also passes sentence. In such cases there are no presentence procedures, and the jury has no information other than the evidence presented at trial upon which to base its decision as to punishment. If, in these states, the defendant waives his right to a jury, the judge may obtain a presentence investigation after his verdict but before he passes sentence.

Punishment

The sentence that a court or jury may impose on a criminal is determined by the legislature, and statues providing particular punishments for particular crimes must be followed. Depending on the law, a court or jury may fine or imprison a criminal or it may do only one or the other. When a person is convicted for several crimes, the sentence may specify that imprisonment for one crime will be served at the same time or "concurrently" with imprisonment for another crime or, as a more severe punishment, one sentence may not begin until after another is finished.

A sentence may be suspended and the convicted criminal placed on probation prior to imprisonment. This is not the same as "parole" which refers to the release of a prisoner before he has completed his full sentence.

The United States Constitution prohibits excessive fines or

"cruel or unusual punishment." Recent decisions of the United States Supreme Court and various state courts have held that the death penalty is "cruel and unusual" under certain circumstances. New legislation is being considered which will deal with the question of the death penalty. Punishments involving torture have long been considered "cruel and unusual," and perhaps society will reach the same conclusion as to the death penalty.

Generally speaking, the punishment must fit the crime. A sentence of life imprisonment for the theft of a bicycle might well be found cruel and unusual. While punishments may differ from one case to the next, they must, under the facts at hand, be applied equally. Thus, punishment for the same crime may change according to the age or criminal record of the guilty, but it may not be based on race or financial condition.

Appeal

A defendant found guilty of a crime may appeal the decision against him. An appeal should be distinguished from a new trial. In many states, a person found guilty of a misdemeanor by a lower court or magistrate is entitled to a new trial at the next highest level. Such a trial is not an appeal since all of the evidence presented in the lower court is heard all over again by the court and, if requested, a jury.

An appeal is a review of what occurred at the trial. The person who "takes" an appeal is known as the appellant. His opponent, the state in a criminal appeal, is the "appellee." The appeal is taken to an "appellate" court.

The basis for an appeal is a claim that, in some respect, a mistake was made at the trial. Frequently this will concern the evidence which the trial judge permitted the state to present in proving its case against the defendant. On appeal, the appellant might claim that the court should not have allowed the jury to consider evidence which the defendant contends was obtained by means of an illegal search. This was the situation in the Texas case we discussed earlier in Chapter 2.

There are many different grounds upon which an appeal may be taken. In civil cases, an appeal may be taken by either side. In criminal law only the convicted defendant may appeal, with a few statutory exceptions.

An appeal can be taken from a final judgment only. If the state introduces evidence that the defendant believes is improper, the case does not stop and an appeal begins. The defendant must object or he loses his right to later complain on appeal that the court made a mistake. When the judge overrules or denies the objection, the lawyer, in most states, "notes his exception" to the court's decision and then the point is "preserved" in the record for later appeal. A failure to do this might mean the point is lost for appeal purposes.

The "record" is just that; it is a word-for-word transcript of everything said at the trial, along with all the evidence that it is introduced by both sides. A court reporter, highly trained to take down each word by means of a stenograph, or, in some cases, a tape machine, is present at every trial. Once a verdict is reached, the defendant, in deciding whether to appeal, reviews the record to decide whether he has a good basis for appeal.

If the defendant decides to appeal, he or she must notify the trial court within a short period of time and may be permitted to remain free on bail or may have to begin serving the sentence. His lawyer, in the meantime, prepares a "brief" describing for the appellate court the points that he claims justify his appeal and referring to the law that supports his claims. The appellee files a brief in opposition.

Thereafter both sides appear before the appeals court to argue their case and answer any questions the court may have. As we said, by appeal, the appellant obtains a review of the trial at which he or she was convicted. No witnesses are heard and no new evidence is offered.

If the appellate court agrees with the appellant, it may do

any of several things. It may reverse the trial court's decision; this means that, instead of guilty, the appellate court says the defendant was innocent, and the trial court is directed to change the verdict accordingly. This might occur where the trial court denied a claim on the defendant's part that he was insane at the time the crime was committed. The appellate court might rule that the evidence clearly proved insanity and the defendant could not be guilty.

When the appeal concerns evidence that the defendant says should or should not have been admitted, the appellate court may order a new trial with directions that the evidence in question must or must not be admitted as claimed by the appellant.

If the appellate court believes that the decision reached in the trial court is correct, it will "affirm" the decision. In the federal system, a second appeal from the Circuit Courts of Appeal may be made to the United States Supreme Court. The Supreme Court, however, is not required to accept the appeal and, when the appeal is denied, the defendant has no further appeal available and must serve his sentence.

In the state courts there are different appeal systems; but, generally, the state's highest court is the final court of appeal. If, in the state courts, a defendant's appeal is denied by the highest state court and his appeal is based upon a denial of a constitutional right, he may be permitted to appeal a state court decision to the federal courts.

What Does Conviction Mean?

A conviction for a felony whether based upon a plea of guilty or a verdict of guilty reached by judge or jury places the individual under a very heavy burden. Beyond the fact that a felon must suffer punishment, his life after he completes his punishment is affected forever. Under early common law, a felony conviction resulted in what was known as "civil death." This meant that the felon lost his civil rights including the right to contract, transfer property and the right to sue. Modern statutes in most states have eliminated such harsh results, but certain limitations still exist.

A convicted felon is frequently denied, by state law, the right to vote. He may not hold public office. If he holds a license to practice as lawyer, doctor, pharmacist or engineer, state law may revoke that license. Certain states and federal law require that felons register periodically and inform certain agencies of their movements.

A felon may be denied a passport, and his conviction, in some states, may be grounds for divorce. When a felon testifies at a trial, the court may instruct a jury that his testimony is subject to question as being untrustworthy. His admission to college graduate school or the armed service may be denied, and employment in civil service or in positions of trust may be denied.

In the view of many, these restrictions are unjust on the theory that a felon who has been sentenced and punished has "paid his debt to society" and can only return to a worthwhile life if his full rights as a citizen are restored. It is difficult to envision true rehabilitation when punishment in one form or another continues for life. Nevertheless, the laws of most states continue to punish after the punishment ordered by the court or jury has been served.

In some cases, more often with the very young or the individual who has demonstrated good citizenship after conviction, a felon may be pardoned and relieved of the many limitations placed upon him. This does not happen often.

Chapter 13

SCHOOL AND THE LAW

As we have stated previously, laws in our country are made to enable us to live in relative freedom. They serve as guides for us so that we will conduct our activities to avoid interference with others. Some laws are in force to enable us to prepare to take full advantage of the privileges, pleasures and opportunities of adulthood. These privileges, pleasures and opportunities are earned by assuming the responsibilities of a good citizen, living within the law and respecting the rights of others.

Some laws relating to education were passed specifically to insure that people receive an education, for their own benefit and that of the country as a whole.

Attendance Required

In most states, young people under a specific age, such as 17 or 18, must attend school until they have achieved a certain grade level, such as grade 9, unless they are excused for special reasons such as problems of physical, mental or emotional health.

To stay away from school without permission is called truancy. A truant can be punished or sent to a special school. Adults guilty of encouraging truancy are also subject to punishment. For example, parents who do not require a child of compulsory school age to attend may be hailed into court and fined or sent to jail. Employers of children who belong in school may be similarly punished. Under certain circumstances, parents may secure special permission to teach their child at home.

Rules and Regulations

Dress and grooming

During recent years, there has been considerable controversy over what authority the public schools have to set rules governing dress, appearance and behavior. There have been arguments put forth that rules and regulations set by some schools deprive students of constitutional rights.

Obviously, a student cannot be deprived of his or her constitutional guarantees upon entering the schoolhouse. In school or out, a person has a right to due process. As we have said, this includes a right to a fair hearing before being convicted or punished for a violation. A law that would punish a person for suspicious behavior would be unconstitutional. School rules and regulations, like laws, must be fair in every case. They cannot be unreasonable or arbitrary.

The courts have recognized that a student has the due process right to notice and hearing prior to expulsion or suspension from school for a substantial period of time.

State laws give public school officials the authority to set the rules governing pupil dress, behavior and appearance. The rules must be reasonable and have a proper public purpose. Extreme styles in dress and hair can be banned if they distract others, create disorder or constitute a danger or discomfort for others. In most cases, the rules seek a balance between private and public interest.

When school rules and regulations have been challenged in the courts, the decisions center on whether they are reasonably justified in terms of the educational program and the rights and freedoms of others.

It would be unreasonable to say that a boy with shoulder length hair could not take shop on the basis that his hair presents a danger to himself in working with machinery if the same regulations permitted a girl with long hair to take shop. It might be reasonable to require both girl and boy to wear a net or tie their hair back.

Student conduct

The laws of the various states govern the behavior of students on school property. Conduct which disrupts classes or interferes with the educational process and atmosphere is punishable. This includes such acts as defacing or destroying school property, marking on walls, making loud noises, or using obscene language. School officials, by state law, are given the authority to adopt and enforce policies, rules and regulations for the conduct of students at school. Students may be suspended, expelled, "kept in" after school or, in most states, subjected to corporal punishment for violation of the rules.

Behavior on the school buses is governed in the same manner as behavior in school, by state law and school policies, rules and regulations. If a student's behavior distracts the bus driver, endangers other students or interferes with their rights, the student may be punished or even arrested for disorderly conduct. If a student on a bus were to behave in such manner as to cause an accident and the death of a pedestrian or another student, the offending student could be subject to the penalties of the "misdemeanor-manslaughter" rule. This merely means that a person who, in the act of committing a misdemeanor (minor crime), causes a death may be convicted for manslaughter.

Loiterers and trespassers

The laws exclude from school property loiterers or persons

who go there to create a disturbance or interference or for other illegal reason. They can be fined or jailed. These laws are aimed at possible drug pushers, kidnappers, sexual perverts, rapists, thieves, gangs who cause trouble, and peddlers of pornographic literature and devices. Students can be helpful in protecting themselves and others by reporting to school or police authorities the presence of such persons on school property.

Hazing

There was a time when "initiating" freshmen into school and initiating persons into student organizations were relatively common practices. So many injuries, even deaths, occurred, that policies that protect students against such practices have been tightened. Any hazing or initiating that causes physical harm is illegal and punishable. Those who conspire to or engage in hazing or any other activity that tends to injure, degrade or disgrace fellow students are subject to punishment.

Discipline and punishment

One of the primary purposes of public education in this country is to help students become responsible, self-disciplined citizens.

But, as yet, no school has been able to operate totally on the basis of each student's self discipline. Some kinds of externally imposed disciplinary measures seem to be required from time to time with some students.

State laws empower principals and teachers to administer reasonable punishment to students who disobey the school rules.

A teacher or principal may punish the student in the same way that a parent would. The punishment must, of course, be reasonable and not cruel or "unusual." The punishment must fit the violation, but, essentially, the laws, though they vary over the country, say that, in school, the teacher stands in the place of the parent in such situations.

The State grants this authority to school officials because they (as agents of the State) are responsible for controlling the conduct of students in order that they will not disrupt classes and the educational atmosphere of the schools or deprive others of their rights or safety. Of course, one of our basic rights is the right to an education and those who, through disruption, interrupt the teaching process are denying others this right.

Decline of in Loco Parentis

In loco parentis—the theory that schools and teachers can exercise control over students because they act in place of the parents and out of concern for students' welfare—has had its challenges and, in effect, has in recent years found lessened support in the courts. The famous Tinker case of 1969 made it clear that *in loco* must yield to the broader concept of the constitutional rights of the individual, whatever his age. The wearing of black armbands by students, according to the court, did not constitute "aggressive, disruptive or even group demonstrations." Rather it involved "direct primary first amendment rights akin to 'pure speech'." It becomes more and more clear that "material disruption" of school affairs or the invasion of others' rights is the somewhat-vague standard by which student actions are judged and not so much as on whether the teacher or administrator happens to find such actions congenial.

Chapter 14

OPERATING AUTOMOBILES AND OTHER VEHICLES

Not so many decades ago, young men (and some young women as well) enjoyed riding a spirited well-groomed horse decked out with matched and ornamental saddle, bridle and martingale or driving such a horse or horses from a "surry with the fringe on top." Back in those days, people were fewer; life was less complex and the pace of travel was slow enough that relatively few traffic laws and regulations were required.

Today the situation is markedly different. Natural horsepower has been replaced by a different kind of horsepower, generated by the combustion of petroleum fuels. Automobiles, trucks, motorcycles, and engine-powered scooters and carts of various kinds have long since replaced the horse. Populations have grown; speed has increased; highways and streets are congested; and, for the safety of the people, laws governing the operation of motor vehicles have become essential.

Licenses

In all our states, anyone who drives or operates a motor vehicle anywhere other than on private property is required by law to have a driver's license. To drive a motor vehicle without a driver's license violates State law. Of course, State laws also require licensing of vehicles.

Securing a Driver's License

Most states permit minors to secure drivers' licenses at age 16. Driving instruction is usually required before a person receives a license, and learners' permits typically are issued to cover the instruction period.

A minor's application to the State Department of Motor Vehicles for a driver's license must, in some States, be endorsed by a parent, guardian, or other adult. Usually, the applicant must pass a written test on the laws and rules of driving as well as an actual driving test.

There are penalties for falsifying a license application, altering a license, lending your license to someone else, or attempting to use another person's license.

Once the applicant for a driver's license secures a learner's permit, he or she has a set period of time to learn to drive. The most popular and a very good way to do this is to take a driver-training course in school. In this way you learn about the automobile and about the laws, rules and codes of driving as well as how to drive, through actual experience. Statistics show that people who learn to drive in this way have fewer accidents than those learning in other ways. They may also qualify for lower insurance rates.

You can have your parents or any other responsible licensed driver teach you to drive. In some States, however, you can be fully licensed at an earlier age if you are a graduate of a school driver-training class.

In many states, licenses contain restrictions requiring persons with weak eyesight to wear corrective lenses and a failure to do so is an offense for which you may be summoned to traffic court.

Traffic Laws and Violations

Every state has extensive laws, rules and regulations governing the use of motor vehicles and prescribes penalties—fines, jail sentences, loss of license or registration—for violations.

Traffic laws vary among the states and, in some respects, from city to city. There has been some agitation to achieve uniform laws through Federal legislation.

Some states have a point system whereby traffic offenders receive a certain number of points for each kind of violation. A driver may lose his driver's license after accumulating a certain number of points.

Drivers committing serious traffic violations are subject to heavy penalties. Licenses may be suspended or revoked for such offenses as failure to stop after an accident, reckless driving, driving under the influence of alcohol or other drugs, failure to properly report an accident or not giving notice of having damaged a parked car. In addition to fines, a jail sentence can be imposed. Persons who have committed traffic offenses generally pay higher insurance rates than drivers with good records and sometimes their insurance is cancelled.

If you are arrested for speeding or another moving violation not serious enough for you to be taken into immediate custody, the officer will ask you to sign a ticket or summons to appear in court. Your signature indicates your agreement to appear. If you refuse to sign, the arresting officer probably will have to take you directly to jail or court. For minor traffic offenses such as overparking, you can usually pay a small fine by mail without appearing in court. For all serious violations, you have to go to court. Also, you have to appear in court if you wish to contest a ticket or prove your innocence.

A traffic ticket, summons or citation calling for you to appear in court will set the date on which you are to appear. When you appear, you may plead "guilty," or "not guilty." If you plead guilty, the judge then has the responsibility to impose a fine, a jail sentence or both. If you plead not guilty, guilt or innocence is determined by trial. The trial may be informal and brief, consisting essentially of the testimony of the police officer and yourself and perhaps a witness; usually there is no jury and the judge will promptly determine your guilt or innocence. In such cases, you have the right of appeal to a higher court. If the offense you are charged with involved an accident, personal injury or property damage, you would be wise to consult a lawyer. If you have witnesses, it is very important that they be present.

A "nolo contendere" plea, explained earlier in Chapter 12, is treated as a guilty plea. However, this plea cannot be used against you as an admission of fault in a subsequent civil suit for damages. Paying a fine without a hearing can, like a guilty plea, be used against you in a civil damage suit. For example, another party to an accident can use your admission of guilt as proof that you were responsible for the accident.

If you, your lawyer or a witness cannot be present on the day you are summoned to appear, you should promptly inform the clerk of the court. You may be required to come to court on an earlier day to request a continuance or postponement to another day. Courts are reluctant to delay trials because, often, the police officer is on a night shift or off duty. You should not wait until your trial date to request a postponement.

Failure to pay your fine or appear in court when required by summons to do so can result in serious penalties, a warrant for your arrest, forfeiture of your driver's license or other penalties.

Traffic Accidents

It is to be hoped that you will never be involved in a traffic accident. Careful driving and strict observance of traffic rules and regulations increase your chances of avoiding accidents. But, if and when you do have an accident, law and common sense dictate what you should do:

1. Stop immediately. Never drive away. Alert oncoming traffic by putting out flares or having someone signal the danger ahead. Notify police and await the arrival of an officer.

2. If anyone is injured, call an ambulance and/or physician. Keep injured people warm. Do not risk injuring people further by moving them, except to free them from such immediate dangers as those posed by fire or oncoming traffic.

3. If another driver is involved, exchange the following information: drivers' license numbers, names, addresses, telephone numbers, make of cars, registration numbers, names of car owners, and names of insurance companies.

4. Write down the time and location of the accident and names, addresses and telephone numbers of everyone involved, including witnesses.

5. If you are dazed or injured in any way, do not make any statements, sign any papers or give any information other than that listed above until you have had medical attention and regained full control of all your senses. You are probably well advised, in any case, to limit your statements to providing the information listed above.

6. As soon as possible, make complete notes of your observations of the accident, how it took place, weather conditions, visibility, signs, traffic signals, and estimated speeds. If possible, take pictures of the cars, debris, skid marks and other evidence.

7. If you are injured in any way, seek a doctor's examination as soon as possible.

8. Notify your insurance company of the accident and fill out all reports required by the police or other law enforcement and governmental agencies. In many States, it is a separate offense *not* to file a report promptly after an accident.

9. Contact your lawyer if anyone was injured or if you were charged with a traffic violation.

10. If the accident involved your damaging parked or unoccupied vehicles or other property, leave a note indicating what happened and listing your name, address, telephone number and car license number. You should also contact the police and report the accident promptly.

One could go on at length describing ways in which vehicle operation is governed by laws and official rules and regulations. For the sake of brevity, here are a few do's and don't's:

1. Don't hitchhike. It is illegal in most States. It is dangerous and often results in crime either by the hitchhiker or driver.

2. Carry liability insurance. Some States require it. *All* require that any driver who causes an accident show evidence of financial responsibility immediately after an accident. This means proof that you are able to pay any damages you may have caused the other persons or their car. Failure to show evidence of financial responsibility could mean your losing your license to drive. Being insured could, in case of an accident, free you of personally having to pay sizeable judgments against you which might keep you financially strapped for years. So carrying insurance (being insured) is vitally important to you.

3. In buying or selling an automobile, be sure that the transfer of ownership is promptly and properly reported to the State. If you do not live in a State that issues titles, be sure to get a bill of sale.

4. In riding bicycles, motorcycles and scooters, observe all traffic signs and regulations. Be sure to have lights if you ride at night—it is dangerous.

5. Never take any motor vehicle without the owner's permission. This is usually classified as larceny, punishable by fine or imprisonment.

6. Avoid "showing off" in a motor vehicle. A driver's scuffling, petting, racing or changing seats while the car is in motion on the streets or highways is not only dangerous but illegal and subject to penalty.

Owning, operating and maintaining motor vehicles are serious responsibilities requiring maturity, good judgment and concern for the other fellow. Every person accepting such responsibility should be sure he or she is ready for it.

Chapter 15

THE TEENAGER IN THE BUSINESS WORLD

Today, many young people, with their parents' encouragement, seek to enter the business world. We have mentioned that a young person's earnings, traditionally, belong to his parents. Many urge their children to gain early experience and responsibility through employment and the handling of money.

In an effort to protect children and their assets, the law limits their ability to contract and frequently requires adult participation in their business ventures. Nevertheless, through programs in school such as distributive education, work experience and Junior Achievement programs, teenagers are taught how to become self-sufficient in the business world. There are many problems which at first appear confusing but which, once faced, turn out to be based on common sense. In this chapter we will cover briefly some areas of the business experience in which you may become involved.

Credit

In most cases in which the business world and the law prevent a minor from contracting, large sums of money are involved. The purchase of a coat, a book or a surfboard certainly all involve contracts, but the fact that the buyer is a minor will will not affect the sale. Such purchases are usually simple cash transactions in which a set sum of money is paid at one time and the goods are taken home.

A majority of people do not have large amounts of money available to pay for expensive things all at one time. A house, farmland, a car or a truck may be necessary for a family or a business but few can manage to set aside through savings the total amount of money required to buy these things when they must have them. To resolve this problem, our society has developed a credit system which enables people to pay for what they want over a period of time.

In its simple day-to-day use, credit is granted by stores to their regular customers. During the course of a month, a customer "charges" his purchases to an account kept by the store or by the use of a charge card issued by a bank. The customer takes his purchase with him but he does not pay for it until after the end of each month when the store or bank adds up all the items charged during the month and sends the customer a bill. In many American households, monthly bill paying is a difficult but necessary task.

Frequently, the cost of a single item is more than a person can set aside in one month. In such cases, the purchase price may be paid over a period of months or years. This most often is accomplished in one of two ways. The purchaser may borrow the money from a lender such as a bank, pay the money over to the seller, and pay the bank back in installments. In such cases, the purchaser has terminated his relationship with the seller once the money is paid over. He has a loan from the bank represented by a "note," which is a document whereby he promises to pay back the amount borrowed within a specified period of time.

In other cases, the purchaser may "finance" his purchase directly with the seller. In such cases, a bank is not involved and the purchaser simply makes periodic payments to the merchant. In either case, the installments are usually equal amounts of money which, when multiplied by the number of payments, amounts to the purchase price, plus interest and any other costs of the sale.

Interest? Costs? What are these things? Whenever money belonging to someone else, such as a bank, or due someone else, such as a store, is paid in installments, an added amount of money, usually a percentage of the total amount, is charged to the borrower for the use of the money. A bank earns its income through interest charged on the loans that it makes.

In terms of contract law, interest is the consideration paid by the borrower for the right to delay paying the full amount borrowed. "Costs" may be an amount charged by the bank for preparing loan documents or, in the case of a store, an administrative expense for maintaining your account.

Let's consider an example of what we have described above. Suppose Gary buys a used car. The purchase price is $1,000.00. Gary has saved $200.00 and the dealer accepts this amount as a "down payment" and agrees to finance the balance at six percent interest over a period of ten months. Each payment will amount to $84.80, $4.80 of each payment being credited toward Gary's interest obligation. This is a very simplified version of how a loan might be financed. The $800.00 might have been borrowed from a bank and paid directly to the dealer, with Gary making his payments to the bank instead.

In either case, the car purchased by Gary would stand as "security" for the loan. This means that, if Gary failed to make his payments, he would lose his car. The dealer or the lender would have a "lien" against the car until the full purchase price, interest and loan costs, were fully paid.

A lien is an ownership interest which a person who sells goods keeps in the property which he sold. It represents a right to take back the property or sell it if the purchaser does not pay what he owes. A person who provides services, such as an automobile repairman or a builder, also can have a lien on the property on which he works.

In most states, liens may be made a public record in a court clerk's office or elsewhere, and such recording is notice to the public that the purchaser does not completely own the property and, therefore, cannot sell it until the lien is paid or the purchaser agrees to assume the responsibilities of the lien.

If a seller "enforces" his lien by retaking possession of the property which he sold, he may then sell it again in an effort to obtain what he has lost through the original purchaser's failure to pay. If, by such a sale, he does not receive the original purchase price, he may sue the original purchaser to make up the difference.

If, on the other hand, all payments are made and the purchase price therefore paid, the purchaser should be certain that the public record of the lien is "released." This means that any notice to the public to the effect that money is owed on a piece of property is eliminated and the purchaser's title to the property is "clear." The law regarding liens varies from state to state. In some cases, a lien does not have to be recorded at all; it is automatic. Thus, an automobile mechanic has a lien for his repair bill and many states provide by law that he can keep the car until his bill is paid. This is known as a "possessory" lien.

Garnishment

When you owe a debt and do not pay it, your creditor may sue you and obtain a judgment for the amount you owe plus the costs of his going to court. If you still do not pay the debt, your creditor may "garnish" your wages. This is a suit filed against your employer which, if successful, requires your employer to pay your earned wages to your creditor. There are strict federal and state laws on garnishment which prevent a wage earner from losing all of his earnings and also prohibit repeated garnishments within specified periods of time. Many employers dislike garnishments because they require the employer to go to court frequently. In some cases, an employer may fire an employee who causes such problems. The law also prevents this in certain circumstances.

Credit Cards

The process whereby a person obtains a credit card, either through a bank or a credit card company, is essentially a contract. Applications for a credit card invariably require the applicant to state his age and, in general, credit cards will not be issued to minors since, as we have noted, their contracts are voidable.

Many states have now passed laws which regulate the use of credit cards. A person who receives a credit card without having applied for one or having consented to its issuance in writing may not be sued for amounts owing through the use of the card in many states. On the other hand, in most states, it is a criminal offense to obtain a credit card through false pretenses, forge a credit card or otherwise use it improperly.

Banks

Banking is a major business in our country. Both state and federal laws strictly control what banks can and cannot do. The reason for this strict control is that most individuals and businesses trust banks to safely keep their money and to pay it out only in accordance with their instructions.

Banks today provide many services. We have referred above to the function of a bank in making loans. Banks also frequently provide advice and guidance to new businesses. They may participate in municipal improvements through bond financing and, frequently, through their "trust departments," they manage funds and property for people who are not familiar with investments and finance. Many banks are participants in credit card operations, issue traveler's checks and otherwise provide services to their community.

Our most frequent relationship with a bank is represented by a "checking account."

Suppose you work for an employer who pays his employees by check. Each payday you receive a small piece of paper which has the name of a particular bank on it. This is a check. It has a date on it and, in printing, says "Pay to the order of," after which is a line with your name on it. At the end of the line is a dollar sign and, in numbers, the amount of dollars you have earned. Beneath it is another line with the same amount written out in words. The check shows the name of your employer and bears his signature or a stamped copy of his signature.

What does the check tell us? Your employer has a "checking account" with the bank named on the check. He has "deposited" or put into the bank an amount of money which the bank is responsible for. They must pay out money as directed by your employer so long as it does not amount to more than he has on deposit.

By your paycheck, your boss says to the bank that, on or after the date filled in, it is to pay you the amount of money shown when you request (order) it. By signing the check on its back, you "endorse" the check and it thereafter may be "cashed." Once you have endorsed the check and given it to the bank teller, the bank is authorized to pay you the amount of money shown on the face of the check.

The bank is responsible to your employer, as it is to all depositors, to be certain that you are the person named on the check. The bank teller may properly request you to identify yourself and, if there are any doubts, he or she may refuse to pay you. The bank must also be certain that your employer's signature is correct and that there are sufficient funds on deposit to pay you.

Now suppose that you have a checking account at the same bank (or at a different bank) and wish to deposit your pay in your account instead of receiving cash for the check. You would fill out a "deposit slip" with your account number on it, showing your employer's check number and the amount of money you wish to deposit. Once presented to the teller, he or she would take the necessary steps to transfer the amount shown on the check from your employer's account to your account. You could then write a check to someone else to whom you owed money and that person could go to the bank and be paid or you could, when you needed money, go to the bank and, by means of a check, "withdraw" the amount required.

When one bank receives a check "drawn" on another bank, it will, if it decides to cash the check, pay out the money and then present the check to the depositor's bank for repayment. You can imagine how many thousands of checks pass between banks as society goes about the day-to-day business of earning salaries and paying its bills.

What we have described above is the normal, regular checking account. Banks offer several different types of accounts. Thus, an account may be in more than one person's name. A husband and wife may have a "joint" account whereby they may each sign checks directing that the bank pay money out of their account. There are savings accounts by which depositors may accumulate funds in a bank and receive interest. This is a percentage of the money in your account at the bank. It is paid to you by the bank for the use of your money. Savings accounts do not involve checks and, therefore, one does not use them in day-to-day financial dealings. A savings account is represented by a passbook which carries a running balance showing the amount of money you have deposited in the account, the balance or total amount of money you have in the account, interest you have earned on the account, and any withdrawals you have made.

Most states have laws which permit minors to open accounts with banks. At the same time, banks are reluctant to open a checking account for unemancipated minors because most young persons do not have a regular income and are not experienced in handling checking accounts. A bank is more inclined to open a savings account for a minor and thereby permit him or her to gain a knowledge of how a bank works. In the event that a minor's parents have a regular account with the bank or if the minor is emancipated and therefore self-supporting, a bank is more likely to permit him or her to open an account. A bank is free to refuse to open an account if it so wishes.

Credit Rating

A "credit rating" is basically one's reputation for meeting financial obligations. If a person does not pay his bills, has been garnished or has had an automobile repossessed, he will undoubtedly have a poor credit rating. On the other hand, the prompt payment of bills, loans and other financial obligations gives one a good credit rating. There are companies whose business it is to gather information regarding a person's credit standing and, for a fee, provide that information to stores which sell to the public. If you wish to open a charge account with a shoe store, you will be asked, usually, to fill out an application for a charge account. This application will ask for your name, address, age, and the name of your employer. In addition, it will request the name of your bank and the names of other companies with whom you have charge accounts. These "references" will be contacted to establish whether you are a good credit risk.

When a person moves to a new town or first reaches adulthood, he may have some difficulty in establishing a credit rating. The first step usually is to open a checking account at a bank. If you use the account properly, maintaining at all times a sufficient deposit to satisfy all checks that you draw on the account, you will begin to establish a good credit rating. This does not happen overnight and you may at first have credit accounts which limit the amount you can charge. Gradually, through sound financial practices, you will develop a reputation upon which others will rely in deciding to extend you credit.

Insurance

Insurance may be generally defined as financial protection against emergencies. An insurance agreement or contract is known as a "policy" and the price paid for the policy is known as a "premium."

Because an insurance policy is a contract, you, as a minor, may be unable to purchase insurance. You will recall that minors can be held responsible for contracts for "necessaries," but it has generally been held, in the case of unemancipated children, that the insurance is not necessary for their support and maintenance. On the other hand, when a young person is emancipated, either through marriage or enlistment in the armed services, insurance, and particularly automobile insurance required by state law, may fall in the category of a necessary.

There are many different types of insurance. Automobile insurance is designed to protect an automobile owner from the damage that may be caused as the result of an automobile accident. Thus, a policy will provide for the payment of medical expenses and other losses sustained by passengers in your car and the driver and passengers in another car if they are injured as a result of your negligence. In addition, the policy will cover necessary repairs to the other car and, if you have "collision" insurance, it may pay for repairs to your own car.

A parent's automobile insurance policy will generally provide coverage, that is, pay damages, for juvenile members of the family who are in the care and custody of the parent. Even though a young family member is away from the home, attending college, he may be protected under the terms of his parent's automobile insurance policy.

The terms of an insurance policy invariably require that the owner of the policy and all persons covered by the policy cooperate with the insurance company. This means that, if you are involved in an accident, you must promptly report the accident to your insurance company and assist in determining what circumstances caused the accident. It may be that a person involved in an automobile accident will be sued for damages caused to the other party. In that event, the insurance company will provide you with an attorney and defend the lawsuit.

Your obligation to cooperate with the insurance company may require you to testify as a witness in the trial. If suit papers are served upon you, you must promptly report this to the insurance company. The failure to do so may free the insurance company from any obligation under the insurance policy. The result could be that you or your parent, the owner of the policy, will have to pay the expenses of the lawsuit and any damages that might be awarded against you.

Traditionally, the recovery of damages by a person injured in an automobile accident is based upon proof that the other party was negligent. Automobile accident lawsuits are actions based upon traditional tort law, which we have discussed earlier. Many state legislatures have now passed, or are strongly considering passing, "no-fault" legislation, which will change the present-day rules applicable to automobile accident cases. No-fault legislation, generally, eliminates proof of negligence as a necessity for the recovery of damages. A person injured in an automobile accident would receive compensation for his injuries regardless of whether the other party to the accident was negligent; and, if he himself had also been negligent, this would not prevent him from recovering compensation.

No-fault laws, both as they have been passed and as proposed in different states, vary widely, and the foregoing is only a general description of this new concept in the field of automobile insurance. One can see, however, that, with the passage of no-fault insurance provisions, much of the expensive litigation and delays now associated with automobile accidents would be eliminated.

Outside the automobile field, there are many other forms of

insurance. Perhaps the most familiar kind of insurance is life insurance. This is insurance which pays a sum of money to the survivors of a person who has died. It is designed to help those survivors who have lost the financial support provided by the deceased. Therefore, quite frequently, life insurance is purchased by the head of a household.

Life insurance costs less if the insured is very young and, for this reason, parents will often purchase life insurance for their children. Generally, when a young person reaches adulthood or thereafter becomes self-supporting, the obligation to pay the life insurance premiums will become his.

The person who receives the proceeds of a life insurance policy upon death is known as a "beneficiary." When parents purchase life insurance for their children, they will generally name themselves as beneficiaries, since it is they who are closest to the child and are paying the premiums. Once adulthood is reached, the child may change the beneficiary by contacting the insurance company. This is usually the case when the child has matured, married and wishes to provide future security for a wife, husband or child.

Another common form of insurance concerns one's property. This will generally provide money to rebuild a house in the event of fire or storm destruction and may also pay damages, should a person be injured while on the insured's property. Insurance may be purchased to protect a business against losses through theft, fire or other casualty. Such a loss might be so severe as to cause the business to close if there were no insurance. Frequently, a company will provide medical insurance for its employees to pay their hospitalization and doctors' bills in the event of injury or illness. It is wise to purchase insurance similar to automobile insurance if you own a boat. In many cases in which an automobile, a motorcycle or a boat is purchased under a financing or loan arrangement, the sales agreement will require that the purchaser maintain a sufficient amount of insurance to protect the seller or the lender against loss. This may include not only insurance protecting the item purchased but could also include life insurance on the purchaser to insure that the full purchase price would be paid in the event something happened to the purchaser.

As stated at the outset, insurance is a form of protection against unexpected financial burdens. Many have decided that, in their particular cases, insurance was not necessary. Many have regretted such decisions, and it is wise to fully analyze any business venture or purchase from an insurance standpoint.

Taxation

Being a minor does not exempt you from income taxes. You must pay federal income taxes on income received by you through employment, from property you own or from property that may be held in trust for you. You must file a federal income tax return if your income exceeds $600.00 during the taxable year. Many states have state income tax requirements, and these also must be followed.

In cases in which a minor's property is held for him by a guardian or trustee, the trustee receives and holds the income from the property and is responsible for paying the minor's taxes.

If the property you own is real estate, you may be required to pay local real estate taxes. These are taxes collected by localities to support public services, such as road maintenance, the operation of schools, and police protection. Again, when the property is managed for you by a guardian, he or she will be responsible for paying the taxes out of income received by the property.

A failure to pay taxes can have serious results. As to income tax returns, a failure to pay or falsifying an income tax return are serious crimes, which can result in fines and imprisonment. In addition, a person is required to pay unpaid taxes, along with penalties and interest. A failure to pay real estate taxes could result in the loss of property.

Chapter 16

LAWYERS AND THE TEENAGER

Why Do You Need a Lawyer?

We have only touched upon several important areas which you might encounter as you enter the business world. There are many others which would add substantially to the length of this book. We cannot anticipate the many legal problems which you might encounter as you reach legal adulthood, but we can suggest a source of help in resolving your legal questions. This source, as the topic indicates, is the legal profession.

A lawyer or attorney is a professional, educated and licensed to provide legal advice and represent the public with regard to its legal problems. With the exception of our lowest courts, and in certain other limited situations in the field of criminal law, a person must have an attorney in order to bring a legal problem before a court or to defend a suit brought against him. Even when there is no legal dispute, a lawyer is frequently necessary to draw a deed, a will, or a business contract. Frequently, through consulting a lawyer, legal problems can be anticipated and avoided.

In our larger cities, lawyers generally practice together in a partnership or a professional corporation, generally referred to as a law "firm." It is not unusual for a law firm in a major city to have 50 or more lawyers, but it is not uncommon either for a lawyer to practice alone.

How Do You Find a Lawyer?

If one has a legal problem and feels that he needs the advice of a lawyer, how does he go about obtaining legal assistance?

Probably you or your family already have an attorney who has provided assistance in the past. He or she will usually be able to help you or, if you have a specialized problem, will be able to send you to an attorney with the experience and background necessary to handle your case. Otherwise, you may turn to a local banker, businessman or your employer, whom you trust, and ask for assistance in obtaining the help of a lawyer. If you are in a strange community and have none of the above resources available to you, there are still reliable means of obtaining an attorney's services. Most lawyers belong to professional organizations, known as "Bar Associations." You will usually find in the yellow pages of the telephone directory under "lawyers" the listing of a service operated by the state or local Bar Association, known as an "Attorneys Referral Service." Through a referral service, the Bar Association will provide you with the name of a local attorney who can handle your problem.

Once you have obtained the name and address of an attorney, you should call his or her office and arrange for an appointment.

What Do You and the Lawyer Need to Know
About Each Other?

Today many attorneys specialize in particular areas of the law just as medical doctors do in one form of medicine or another. There are doctors whose abilities are devoted to child care or pediatrics, or problems involving injuries to bones or nerves. Likewise, there are attorneys who specialize only in such fields as taxation, business law, or divorce. You should be certain, on meeting your attorney, that he is able to handle your particular problem. Many lawyers are general practitioners, fully capable of handling most problems that are brought to them. If they are not, they will properly refer you to the specialist you need.

In discussing your problem with a lawyer, you must understand that his services depend to a great extent upon your giving him all of the information concerning your particular legal problem. This may involve revealing embarrassing personal information, which you do not wish disclosed to others. Your relationship with your lawyer is confidential, and he is bound to protect your confidences in all cases, except when it might involve him in a criminal act.

How Are Lawyers Paid?

Lawyers in the United States are usually paid in one of two ways. When you wish to sue another person for injuries which you have suffered, either to your person or to your property, the lawyer may enter into a contract with you whereby he will receive as his fee a percentage of the money you recover through your lawsuit. This is known as a "contingent fee" agreement. Usually, an attorney's fee in such cases amounts to between one-quarter and one-third of the amount of damages recovered. Thus, a jury may award you $900.00 in damages and, of that sum, you will pay $300.00 to your attorney for his services. The contingent fee arrangement is most frequently found in negligence lawsuits in which personal injuries are involved.

In the field of business law, wills, and in cases which do not necessarily involve litigation, lawyers are frequently compensated on an hourly basis. Thus, an attorney may charge a certain amount for each hour he works on your particular legal problem. An attorney operating on this basis keeps strict account of his time and can provide you with a summary of his hours, should you request it.

In representing you, a lawyer will incur certain expenses. These may include bills for long-distance phone calls, hiring the services of a surveyor, an accountant, or an expert witness, or in paying charges necessary to the filling of a lawsuit and the summoning of witnesses. These expenses are outside of, and in addition to, the fee owed the lawyer for his services.

In some cases today a law firm may charge a "flat fee" for purely routine matters such as a simple will or an uncontested divorce. It is difficult however to anticipate what is routine and what is not. Often a complex problem develops out of a simple situation. One should always ask a lawyer at the outset what his charges are and for an estimate of how much his help will cost in your case.

In many cases, a lawyer will inform his client as to the fee and require at least a partial payment of the fee before agreeing to take the case. This is known as a "retainer."

Lawyers in criminal practice base their fees upon their past experience in handling similar cases and upon their skill and ability as successful criminal lawyers. There are few lawyers who win every criminal case and many have learned from sad experience that, once convicted, a criminal defendant often shows little concern for his lawyer's bill. For this reason, a lawyer in a criminal case may insist upon full payment of his fee before trial.

Who Sets Ethical Standards for the Law Profession?

As with all professions, there are individual lawyers in the legal profession who behave in a dishonorable manner. In spite of a strict code of ethics, the violation of which may lead to the loss of a lawyer's license, there are those who, for their own personal gain, ignore the standards by which their profession is governed. Bar Associations, both national and local, are constantly working to rid the profession of those unscrupulous few who, through their conduct, damage the reputation of all lawyers. A person seeking legal advice must be cautious, nevertheless.

A lawyer must not solicit your business nor have others solicit cases on his behalf, and you should beware of persons who appear to have a relationship with an attorney whereby they receive compensation for sending you to his office. A lawyer may not advertise except in a limited way, giving his name, address and the amount he charges for routine matters. He may not take cases wherein he represents conflicting interests. A lawyer's obligation is first and foremost to his client, and he may only compromise or settle a case in his client's best interest and with his client's full and knowledgeable consent. In the event a lawyer behaves contrary to the ethical standards of his profession, he should be reported to the State or local Bar Association.

It is frequently said that the legal profession's greatest skill lies in its ability to overcomplicate a simple situation. Lawyers are familiar with problems that quite frequently develop if their advice is ignored or a client, frustrated by delay, decides to take his representation into his own hands. Much publicity is given to trials and the courts, but it is a lawyer's obligation, you must remember, to avoid legal disputes. A well-drawn will or contract, a settlement which avoids expensive and time-consuming litigation, or a deed which fully protects the title of a purchaser invariably represents the best that the legal profession can offer.

Chapter 17

SUMMARY AND CONCLUSION

The Law Protects Our Freedom

Every one of us should realize that the law exists for our convenience, to enable each of us to enjoy the most freedom possible.

We are free to express opinions and ideas, worship as we please, take stands and support causes, move about as we wish and do scores of other things at will. We're so free that we seldom take time to appreciate the high degree of liberty we do enjoy.

But we do have limitations. We must not, in our expression of freedom, interefere with the freedom of others. The law tells you when, where and how to limit your activities to avoid such interference and sets penalties for your failure to heed the legal requirements.

The Law Conforms to Our Needs

The law follows us around. It adapts to our needs. The energy crisis of the seventies was not fully foreseen. When it arrived, we faced new problems. Laws were enacted to regulate our behavior and insure the greatest possible convenience and the least possible curtailment of freedom for all of us.

The Law Reflects Our Wishes

Laws are not created in a vacuum. They reflect the public will. Any law opposed by the majority of the people cannot long stand in a democratic society.

Sometimes the laws say things an individual dislikes. But one can be quite sure that such resentment is not general or the law would be changed. We make the laws.

It is the obligation of each of us, in assuming the responsibilities of citizenship, to live within the law, respecting the rights of others at all times.

Changing the Law

When a law appears to be unfair, it can be changed. That change, however, should be sought by legal means only. In a land like ours, in which matters are determined by all the people and in the interest of all the people, no individual can have things all his way all the time. Change may be gradual to the extent that reform often means a change of elected officials, and this takes time. The election process, however, enables all of us to be "heard" through our vote and, in most cases, leads to intelligent, constructive change, reflecting the will of the majority while protecting the interests of the minority.

Rules of thumb for governing our activities

Sound judgment and consideration for others are most helpful to anyone wishing not to run afoul of the law.

Nobody should have to tell us not to engage in activities which:

—interfere with the disciplined operation of community life and the free movement of its people.

—disrupt the activities of others or promote disorder.

—invade the rights of others or deprive them of their property or the use thereof.

—are obscene or harmful to the sensitivities of most people.

—involve false statements which may subject others to hatred, ridicule, contempt or injury.

—involve statements grossly unfair or prejudicial to anyone.

One could easily extend the list. It is not intended to be all-inclusive. Its purpose is merely to remind us that, in return for the freedoms and privileges each of us is guaranteed in our country, we have the responsibility to respect the rights and property of all other persons.

One of the most important evidences of true maturity in an individual is self-discipline in observing the privileges of others and adherence to legitimate rules and regulations adopted for the common good.

Basic Purpose of the Book

This little book deals with a very complex subject. It is not intended to make lawyers of its readers or even to serve as a do-it-yourself law course. If the reader is helped to be more aware of his or her rights and responsibilities and legal obligations and has gained respect for our legal system, it has accomplished its purpose.

GLOSSARY

Accounts Receivable: Debts due a person or a business, generally for purchases.

Admissible: Generally refers to evidence presented at a trial, acceptable and proper for the court or jury to consider in reaching a decision.

Adultery: Voluntary sexual intercourse by a married person with another who is not the married person's husband or wife.

Adversary: An opponent; two persons opposing each other are adversaries.

Advocate: One who assists, advises, defends and argues for another person; usually a lawyer licensed to act in a court to represent a person in a lawsuit.

Affidavit: A written statement of facts given voluntarily and under oath.

Annul: To make void or of no effect; as if the act in question never happened; annulment: the process by which an act is declared void.

Appeal: In a lawsuit, the step whereby a higher court is asked to review the decision of the trial court, the appellant or person appealing usually basing his appeal on a claim that a mistake was made in the trial of the case.

Appellate Court: A court which reviews the decision of a lower court at the request of a person who is dissatisfied with the lower court's decision and which has the power to change or approve the decision.

Arraignment: In a criminal case, the act by which the accused is read the charge against him and asked whether he wishes to plead innocent or quilty.

Arrest: To take one's liberty by legal authority; to take custody or control of a person legally.

Assets: Generally, a person's property; that which can be used for the payment of a person's debts.

Bail: Security, either of money or a promise to pay money called a bail bond, deposited with a court to obtain the release of a person under arrest until he or she is brought to trial. If the person does not appear for trial the money is forfeited to the court.

Bar: Traditionally, a part of the courtroom separated from the public area where only judges, lawyers and officers of the court could go. Today it refers to lawyers generally, those licensed and "admitted to practice," that is, those who can legally act as lawyers; the Bar. Organizations for lawyers are known as Bar Associations.

Beneficiary: One who benefits as the result of an agreement or an act done, usually by someone else. The beneficiary of a trust is the person who receives property or income from a trust. The beneficiary of a life insurance policy receives income upon the death of the insured person.

Bequeath: To give, through a will, personal property such as jewelry, furniture or money to another person.

Bigamy: Marrying a second time without the first marriage having been legally ended by death, divorce or annulment.

Bill: In law, a statement in writing setting forth a claim against another to be filed in a court to start a lawsuit; a complaint, claim, or cause or motion for judgment.

Bill of Sale: In contract law, a written agreement by which a person transfers to another person his or her ownership interest in property, usually personal property such as an automobile rather than real property which is tranferred by deed.

Bond: A certificate, document, or other writing that establishes or stands for a debt; to "post" bond is to give a bond or promise to pay if certain duties are not performed properly.

Breach: To break or fail to carry out in accord with a contract; a contract or agreement can be breached by failing to perform one's obligations or by performing one's obligations incorrectly.

Breach of the Peace: A criminal offense, usually a misdemeanor, sometimes known as disturbing the peace or disorderly conduct by which a person or group in one way or another violates the normally peaceful atmosphere; to disturb or bother one's neighbors.

Canon: A disciplinary rule usually designed to govern the conduct of a particular group. Canons are derived from church law or canon law but today, for example, lawyers are governed by canons of ethics designed to set forth what lawyers can or cannot do.

Capital Offenses: In criminal law, those crimes for which a person may be sentenced to death, known as capital punishment, or life imprisonment.

Case: A general term to describe a legal dispute brought before a court; an action, a suit, a cause or a cause of action.

Chain of Title: The history of the ownership of property showing chronologically each successive owner.

Citation: (1) An order issued by a court directing a person to come to court or "appear" at a particular time and place. (2) In legal writing, reference to the name or title of a case or a statute and book and page number where it can be found.

Cite: (1) To direct a person to do something, usually to come to court on a particular date. (2) To refer to a particular legal case or a law which applies to a problem being considered by a court, see citation.

Civil Case: A dispute between citizens that does not involve a crime.

Civil Disobedience: A term describing non-violent behavior which violates a law, usually for the purpose of testing the law's validity in court when the violator is brought to trial.

Civil Law: In general, the law concerning conduct or disputes of a non-criminal nature between citizens; historically, it refers to the law that originated in Roman times and is now used and applied in Europe and, in America, in the State of Louisiana.

Civil Rights: The rights held by all citizens.

Code: A collection of laws.

Consideration: In contracts, that which is given in exchange for what one receives from another. If a pen costs $2.00 that amount is the consideration you must pay for the pen. If, on the other hand, you are selling the pen, then the pen itself is the consideration you must give when you are paid the $2.00.

Contingent Fee: In civil cases compensation paid a lawyer that depends on the success of the lawsuit. Thus, if a lawyer and his client agree upon a 25% contingent fee and the client recovers $400.00, the lawyer is paid $100.00. If the case is lost, the lawyer receives nothing.

Continuance: The postponement of a trial date; if a trial or hearing is rescheduled for a later date it is said that the trial is continued; also adjournment.

Contract: An agreement between two or more persons; an exchange of promises. A contract may be verbal or written.

Contributory Negligence: A lack of care on the part of the person who is injured, which combined with someone else's carelessness, caused the injury complained of. A person who ignores a stop light and is struck by a speeder is contributorily negligent.

Conviction: In a criminal case, the decision of the court or jury that the accused person is guilty of the charge against him or her.

Corporal Punishment: Physical punishment where something

is done to the person's body; it may include whipping or imprisonment.

Court: A branch of the government established to decide disputes by trial between citizens or to administer justice by trial to citizens charged with breaking the law; presided over by a judge and frequently involving the use of a jury; also, a place where trials take place.

Creditor: A person to whom money is due or owing; a debt holder.

Criminal: One who has been convicted of a crime; one who has been found by a court to be legally guilty of committing a crime.

Criminal Case: A case that is begun by the government's charging a person with breaking the law.

Curfew: A set time established, usually by city ordinance, after which certain persons must leave the public streets and go to their homes, usually applied to minors nowadays.

Damages: Money which is requested in a lawsuit as compensation for an injury or the breach of an obligation by another person; also, the money that is actually awarded by the court or jury as compensation in civil cases.

Debt: A sum of money that is due under the terms of an agreement or contract.

Debtor: A person who owes a debt, usually money, to a creditor.

Decree: The judgment or decision of a court in an equity case such as a divorce or an injunction.

Deed: A written agreement by which the ownership of land is transferred from one person to another.

Defendant: A person who is charged with a duty or violation of the law in a lawsuit and who must defend the charges or claims against him or her.

Delinquency: The violation of a law; the failure to perform a duty or meet an obligation. As applied to a debt or contract, the term may refer to a failure to perform a duty on time; lateness.

Divorce: The process by which a marriage is ended. Divorce is an equitable remedy provided for by state law which ends a marriage. It may determine the ownership of property belonging to the divorced husband and wife and make provision for the support and custody of any children of the marriage.

Docket: A record of all acts done by a court; in some courts it is a schedule or calendar of cases set for trial. Used as a verb, it means to schedule a case for trial on a certain date.

Domicile: The place where a person has his permanent home and to which he means to return.

Double Jeopardy: Charging and prosecuting a person more than once for the same crime.

Due Care: In tort law; reasonable behavior under the circumstances presented; conduct which is not negligent.

Due Process: Following properly the procedures established by the constitution and the laws in determining a person's right to property and freedom.

Dunning Letter: A letter sent to a debtor insisting that a debt be paid and usually warning of legal action unless payment is made.

Duress: Unusual pressure directed at a person to compel him to do a certain thing against his natural will; not necessarily involving physical force but may include threats of harm.

Eminent Domain: The power of a government to take private property for public use.

Equity: A broad term which, when applied to the activity of a court, concerns an action or case brought to require that something be done or that something that is being done be stopped. It refers and is based on morals and fairness. In the law of property, the term is used to mean ownership.

Estate: All of the property in which an individual has an ownership interest. A person's estate may consist of land, personal property such as a boat or livestock, cash, jewelry or books, or intangible property such as debts owed to her or him, stocks or a share in a business.

Evidence: Proof in any of many forms including writings, verbal testimony, objects, or actions legally accepted at a trial to persuade a jury or the court that certain claims are valid or invalid.

Exchange: To barter, trade or swap.

Execute: In reference to legal documents, to sign or complete a writing; in criminal law, to put to death.

Exhibit: A writing or an object admitted at a trial as evidence of a fact or facts.

Expert Evidence: Testimony presented at a trial by a specialist in a particular field who by reason of his training, education or experience is particularly qualified and may express an opinion as to certain facts and their meaning.

Fact: That which actually happened or existed.

False Arrest: The unlawful holding or keeping of a person, against his or her will, in prison or elsewhere.

Fee: A charge fixed by law to be paid for the services of a public official such as a clerk of court or a sheriff; also, the amount charged by a lawyer for his services.

Felon: A person who commits a felony.

Felony: A crime, more serious than a misdemeanor; generally a felony is an offense for which the maximum penalty is death or life imprisonment.

Fiduciary: A person or an institution which acts on behalf of another and in whom trust is placed. A trustee is a fiduciary in whom the care and well being of a person or a person's property is entrusted.

Firm: A group or company formed to conduct a business; a law firm is a group of lawyers who work together, have a common office and a single name that may include all or some of the names of the lawyers in the firm.

Fiscal Year: An accounting period of twelve months, not necessarily the same as the calendar year, at the end of which an accounting is generally made.

Forfeit: To lose, give up or pay over something of value as a result of neglect or wrongdoing.

Forgery: Falsely writing or altering something written for the purpose of committing fraud or gaining property or money that belongs to someone else.

Foster Parents: A man and a woman who raise the children of others and who have the authority and duties of a father and a mother.

Fraud: Intentional deception or misleading to gain an advantage over another or to obtain the property of another; cheat or trick.

Garnishment: A legal process whereby money or property due a debtor by another person is taken to satisfy the debtor's obligations. If John owes Sally $10.00 and Sally owes Maria $10.00, Maria may, after proving that Sally owes her the money, proceed by garnishment to make John pay her. In paying Maria, both John's and Sally's debts are satisfied.

Guarantee: A promise to pay or do something if another person fails to; to vouch for the quality of a thing or the ability of a thing to perform as it was meant to.

Guaranty: A written pledge by which a person becomes responsible for the payment of a debt or the performance of an obligation by another person.

Guardian: One who has the legal responsibility for another person who for some reason is unable to be responsible for himself or herself.

Guardian Ad Litem: A guardian who is appointed by a court with respect to a particular case or proceeding for the purpose of protecting the interests and rights of a person who is legally incapable of self-protection.

Hearing: A proceeding before a court usually to consider a particular question or issue in connection with a lawsuit; frequently used as a synonym for a trial in an equity case.

Hearsay: Something one has heard but does not know to be true; rumor; gossip.

Heir: One who is entitled to receive or inherit the property of a person who has died.

Homicide: The killing of a human being.

Hourly Fee: Compensation paid a lawyer based upon a set rate for each hour he or she spends working on a client's case.

Illegal: Not permitted by law; unlawful, illicit.

Indictment: A written accusation under oath by a grand jury charging a person with a crime.

Information: A written accusation issued by a government official under oath, usually a district attorney or other law officer, charging a person with a criminal offense.

Infant: In legal terms, a minor, one who has not yet reached the age of majority.

Inherit: To legally receive the property of another person who has died.

Inheritance: The property which an heir legally receives or inherits from a person who has died.

Injunction: In a case in equity, a court order directing that something be done, a mandatory injunction, or directing that something that is being done be stopped.

In loco parentis: In the place of a parent.

Insolvent: Unable to pay one's debts.

Installments: Periodic partial payments. A borrower may pay back a loan of one hundred dollars in four installments of twenty-five dollars each.

Insurance Policy: The written contract between an insured and the insurance company which sets forth the risks covered, the period of time covered during which the insurance company is obligated to pay and the amount the insured must pay for the policy.

Intent: Purpose; a mental attitude involving the knowledge of what the results of an act will be.

Interest: In property law, a general term to describe a person's rights as to certain property. As to a loan, interest is the amount of money a borrower pays a lender for the use of the borrower's money in addition to the principal amount of the loan.

Intestate: Without a will; a person who dies without having made a will is described as having died intestate.

Irrelevant: Information that does not relate to a question before the court or jury. Irrelevant evidence does not prove or disprove a fact and it is inadmissible as evidence at a trial.

Jeopardy: At risk, in hazard or danger.

John Doe: The name assigned to an unknown person or a person whose true name is unknown.

Joint: Referring to two or more persons acting together or having a common interest; a joint bank account is one in which two or more persons have the right to deposit and withdraw money.

Judgment: The decision of a Court.

Judiciary: The system of courts including both the trial and the appellate courts; its judges and the administrators of the court system; a branch of government.

Jurisdiction: The authority or power of a court; the scope of a court's authority to decide a case.

Juvenile Court: A court having jurisdiction over minors.

Landlord: The owner of land or buildings who leases or rents to others known as tenants in return for which he is paid money or rent.

Larceny: Illegally taking the property of another person for the purpose of keeping it.

Lease: A contract between a landlord and a tenant that may be in writing or verbal. It contains the terms of their agreement.

Legitimate: Lawful, recognized and permitted by law.

Liability: Generally a debt or an obligation; a duty to pay or meet a responsibility imposed by the law or by a court.

Libel: Writing that damages the reputation or otherwise injures another person. Libel is a civil wrong in the law of torts.

License: A document granting authority to do some act such as operate an automobile, practice medicine, conduct a bingo game or hunt wildlife; permission granted by a government.

Lien: A claim against a piece of property generally based upon work done on the property or money lent to the property owner for the purpose of buying, repairing or improving the property.

Loiter: To stand idle, linger without apparent purpose.

Magistrate: An officer of the court often having authority to decide restricted legal questions and issue warrants for arrest.

Malice: Intending by a wrongful act to cause injury to another.

Malpractice: The failure on the part of a professional such as a lawyer, doctor or architect to exercise his particular skill properly.

Manslaughter: The unlawful killing of another without prior plan or intent. Manslaughter may be voluntary or involuntary. In some states manslaughter is broken down into degrees. First degree manslaughter may, in such cases, be murder and in such a case refer to a planned killing. Second degree manslaughter would refer to voluntary manslaughter as in the case where a person is killed in anger in the course of a fight. Third degree manslaughter might refer to involuntary manslaughter as in the case of a person darting in front of a moving automobile.

Misdemeanor: A crime that is less serious than a felony and for which the punishment is not as severe.

Motion: In law, a request that the court make a decision on a particular question.

Murder: See manslaughter.

Negligence: Doing that which a normal reasonable person would not do; carelessness. A failure to use ordinary care under the particular circumstances presented.

Nolo contendere: The name of a plea in criminal law whereby the defendant rather than plead guilty or innocent says, "I will not contest the charge." Legally it is the same as a plea of guilty.

No-fault Insurance: A term used to describe a system of automobile insurance under which a person who is injured will be paid for his damages whether or not the injured person or the person causing the injury was negligent.

Notary public: A public officer authorized to administer oaths and to perform certain other official acts.

Note: A written promise to pay a certain sum of money at a specified time and place to a person named in the note or, if the note is payable to "bearer", to whoever has the note.

Oath: A spoken or written pledge made before a public officer attesting or promising that the statements made are the truth. A person giving an oath is often described as having "sworn" to tell the truth.

Obligation: In legal terms, a legal promise to do something; a legal duty.

Offense: A crime or misdemeanor in violation of criminal laws.

Opinion: A written statement by a judge giving the reasons for a judgement.

Parole: In criminal law, the release of a prisoner on the condition that he or she behave properly, obey the law and, if required, report periodically to a parole officer.

Party: A person taking part in a lawsuit as either plaintiff or defendant or who participates in a contract, loan or other legal transaction.

Perjury: The crime of knowingly failing to tell the truth under oath either in a trial or, if a statute so provides, in signing a document one knows to be false such as a tax return.

Plaintiff: The person who begins a lawsuit stating a claim against another person. A person who legally complains that he has suffered a wrong.

Plea: In criminal law, the answer of a defendant to a charge against him.

Pleadings: The writings exchanged in a lawsuit by the plaintiff and the defendant, filed with the clerk and generally responding to the claims set forth in the pleadings of the opposing party.

Political rights: Those rights which a citizen has with respect to the government under which he lives.

Poll Tax: A tax required in years past as a condition for the right to vote.

Pornography: Literature which is generally considered obscene, that is describing sexual encounters and using language in a manner that is unacceptable to the general public. Obscene writing or pictures.

Possessory lien: A creditor's claim whereby the property may be kept by the creditor until the debt is paid. In many states a mechanic may keep possession of an automobile until the bill for repairs is paid; the mechanic has a possessory lien.

Precedent: A decision by a court which provides an example for other courts to follow in similar cases.

Premium: The amount charged by an insurance company for an insurance policy.

Presentment: The written statement of a grand jury's accusation or indictment charging one with the commission of a crime.

Probate: The process whereby a will is presented to a clerk of a court for the purpose of proving that it is the only true will of a person who has died. When there is a challenge to the will's validity, or other wills are also presented, a will "contest" or hearing will be held, often in a probate court to decide the dispute.

Prosecutor: The public official who represents the government in proceedings against a person charged with a crime; having various titles such as district attorney, commonwealth's attorney, attorney general or, in the federal courts, United States Attorney.

Recognizance: A promise without security or bail bond by a person accused of a crime that he or she will be present in court on a certain date at a certain time and place.

Recovery: The amount or things ultimately given by the judgment of a court to a successful party.

Release: A written agreement whereby a person gives up particular rights against another in return for payment.

Removal: As to a lawsuit, the transfer of a case from one court to another.

Retainer: As to the employment of lawyers, an amount of money paid to the attorney at the time he is first hired or "retained". In paying a retainer a person assures that the lawyer will represent no other party in the dispute.

Sentence: The formal judgment of a court in a criminal case setting forth the convicted criminal's punishment.

Settlement: The voluntary adjustment or compromise of a dispute; payment and acceptance of payment prior to the filing of a lawsuit; or, if after filing, prior to the decision of a judge or jury.

Sue: To begin a legal action; file suit.

Summons: An order or notice to a person to appear before a court or judge at a certain time and place to answer a charge or a claim against him or her.

Surrogate's court: The name given in some jurisdictions to courts dealing with wills and estates; probate court.

Swear: To place a person under an oath to tell the truth.

Teller: An employee in a bank who takes in and pays out money.

Title: A word having many meanings; in law it is frequently used to refer to ownership, possession or the right to possess and control. The title to an automobile is the document proving ownership. "Good title" refers to ownership as to which there are no legal questions.

Tort: A non-criminal wrong; the violation of obligations owed others aside from contracts, such as the obligation or duty to operate an automobile safely.

Trust: An arrangement whereby property is held by a person, known as a trustee, for another person's benefit.

Valid: Legally correct and of binding effect. A valid contract is one that is not subject to question and must be followed.

Verdict: The decision or finding of a unanimous jury as to the question put to it by the court; in a criminal case, whether the defendant is guilty or innocent; in a civil case, whether the defendant is or is not liable, or responsible.

Void: Having no legal effect, that which cannot be enforced; null, unenforceable.

Waiver: The voluntary giving up of a right.

Ward: A person, frequently a minor, who is legally under the control and protection of a guardian or a court.

Warrant: An order issued by a court directing a sheriff or similar official to arrest a person or do some other act. Similarly, a writ or order giving authority to do something.

INDEX